DINING AND THE
OPERA
IN MANHATTAN

Sharon O'Connor's Menus and Music

DINING AND THE

OPERA
IN MANHATTAN

Recipes from Manhattan Restaurants

Opera Arias Selected by the Metropolitan Opera Guild

Menus and Music Productions
Emeryville, California

An American Place recipes on pages 17-22 are from *An American Place* by Larry Forgione, published by William Morrow, New York

The Four Seasons recipes on pages 59-65 are from *The Four Seasons* published by Addison-Wesley Publishing, New York

Library of Congress Cataloging-in-Publication Data
O'Connor, Sharon
Menus and Music Volume VIII
Dining and the Opera in Manhattan
Recipes from Manhattan Restaurants
Opera Arias Selected by the Metropolitan Opera Guild

Includes Index
1. Cookery 2. Entertaining
I. Title
94-078254
ISBN 1-883914-03-5 (paperback)
ISBN 1-883914-04-3 (hardcover)

Menus and Music is published by

Menus and Music Productions, Inc.
1462 66th Street
Emeryville, CA 94608
(510) 658-9100

Book and cover design by Michael Osborne Design, Inc.
Cover photograph by Paul Franz-Moore
Inset cover photograph by Frank Dunand courtesy of the Metropolitan Opera
Guild Education Department

Manufactured in the United States of America
10 9 8 7 6 5 4 3

Contents

Foreword

Dining and the Opera in Manhattan—what images of wonder and delight this title conjures up! I cannot imagine any finer combination for an evening's enjoyment than the splendor of grand opera combined with a gourmet repast at one of Manhattan's (and by natural extension, therefore, one of the world's) finest restaurants. Menus and Music and the Metropolitan Opera Guild have joined forces to bring this marvelous combination into your home.

The fabulous art of opera expresses the full range of human emotion with enormous power yet infinite delicacy, all through the universal language of music and song. It is the most splendid of entertainments—a true feast for the ears, the eyes, and the soul. The program of arias and ensembles offered here is only a tiny taste of opera's many glories, but it is a truly lovely sample and I am pleased to be a part of it as one of the recording's featured performers.

Of course, man does not live by opera alone, and these marvelous recipes from twenty-one of my hometown's finest eateries are ample proof of the great harmonies that can be produced by wonderful food and music. Enjoy!

— Beverly Sills

Introduction

Opera and fine dining, both dear to the romantics of the world, are two of life's great pleasures. As America's most vibrant metropolis, Manhattan sets a standard of excellence and is the zenith of opera and fine dining. This volume combines the cultural tradition of the Metropolitan Opera and the culinary artistry of twenty-one acclaimed Manhattan restaurants.

This project was originally suggested by the Metropolitan Opera Guild, who saw the *Menus and Music* series as a way of presenting opera to a wider audience. Created for people who enjoy the strong affinity between food and music, this book and its accompanying musical program have been a rewarding exchange of talent and expertise.

The musical program recorded here has been carefully selected to include Italian, French, German, and American opera favorites. It can be enjoyed while cooking, during festive or romantic dining, or as a beautiful after-dinner concert. These arias are for enjoyment by ardent opera fans, those just learning to enjoy the magic and mystery of grand opera, and people who simply like beautiful music. The performances, by some of the world's most celebrated opera singers, are exceptional by any standard.

I asked chefs from twenty-one Manhattan restaurants to create a menu and recipes in celebration of opera and The Met. I had the luxury of choosing from many fine restaurants in Manhattan, many more than could possibly be included. The chefs composed their menus anticipating a musical accompaniment of opera arias. Italian chefs were inspired to create pasta dishes to celebrate their love of Puccini, a French pastry chef developed a recipe for Opera Cake, and an all-American Apple and Cranberry Duff is included for George Gershwin.

I am honored and pleased to have made the acquaintance of so many accomplished and innovative chefs during the past year. While creating this volume, I enjoyed many unforgettable experiences. There was an amazing discussion about food and philosophy with a French chef at his four-star restaurant, which

7

Introduction

was filled with celebrities and fashionable patrons. I'll never forget a lengthy conversation with a gifted young chef about his mentor and the pursuit of perfection as he guided me through a four-course meal, explaining ingredients and how each dish was made. One chef came from his kitchen to bring me recipes written by hand in Italian, while another gave me a tour of his kitchen and explained the various work stations and types of equipment during a lull before the dinner crowd arrived. At one point there were almost daily phone conversations with chefs and pastry chefs concerning ingredients, elaborations on shorthand cooking notations, and various other recipe explanations. These twenty-one chefs will provide you with a connoisseur's guide to dining in Manhattan. I know you will appreciate their talent, expertise, and creativity.

You can re-create an entire menu from this book or choose dishes from several restaurants to create your own sampler. The chefs have provided you with a chance to savor Cream of Basil Soup from La Côte Basque, Lobster Maccheroni with Balsamic Vinegar from Palio, Veal Chops Grand-mère from Café des Artistes, and Crème Brûlée from Le Cirque. The plenitude of available foods at the market makes cooking these diverse dishes in your home kitchen possible. Line up the ingredients in advance and prepare food ahead of time as much as possible. You can mix and match the recipes with your own favorites or create your own menu as long as you achieve a balance of tastes. This book includes some luxuries that require rationing; they are for special occasions, but when that occasion comes, enjoy every mouthful!

Creating this volume has been a pleasure and a privilege. I hope it encourages you to enjoy great music and food together. Whether you are planning an intimate supper or a festive dinner party, an accompaniment of beautiful opera arias will give the evening a real sense of occasion. You'll be sure to hear a few bravos!

— *Sharon O'Connor*

Music Notes

Così Fan Tutte, first performance 1790
Wolfgang Amadeus Mozart (1756–1791)
"Soave sia il vento"
Leontyne Price, Tatiana Troyanos, Ezio Flagello
New Philharmonia Orchestra, Erich Leinsdorf

In late eighteenth-century Naples, two young noblemen decide to test the fidelity of their respective fiancées by pretending to go away on campaign then returning in disguise, each to woo the betrothed of the other. After the young men take their leave and sail away, the two young women, along with an elderly bachelor, Don Alfonso, sing a prayer for the wind to carry their loved ones safely to their destination.

Der Rosenkavalier, first performance 1911
Richard Strauss (1864–1949)
"Mir est die Ehre" (The Presentation of the Rose)
Risë Stevens, Erna Berger
RCA Victor Orchestra, Fritz Reiner

In eighteenth-century Austria, the young cavalier Octavian (a role sung by a woman) has come to the home of Sophie von Faninal to offer her a silver rose, a traditional symbol of love that does not fade, in token of a proposal of marriage for one of his kinsmen. He is unaware that, in the process, he will fall hopelessly in love with Sophie himself, and she with him.

Die Zauberflöte (The Magic Flute), first performance 1791
Wolfgang Amadeus Mozart (1756–1791)
"Bei Männern, welche Liebe fühlen"
Ileana Cotrubas, Christian Boesch
Vienna Philharmonic Orchestra, James Levine

In an imaginary kingdom beyond time and space, the princess Pamina sings a delightful duet with Papageno, the bird catcher, who has come with

Pamina's beloved, Prince Tamino, to rescue her from captivity. They sing in praise of love, the greatest good, which they both seek.

Faust, first performance 1859
Charles Gounod (1818–1893)
"Salut! demeure chaste et pure"
Plácido Domingo
New Philharmonia Orchestra, Nello Santi

Faust, an aged philosopher in medieval Germany, has regained his youth in a pact with Mephistopheles. Pursuing the lovely young Marguerite, Faust pauses before her home, saluting it as a shrine that embodies all the beauty and innocence of his beloved.

Gianni Schicchi, first performance 1918
Giacomo Puccini (1858–1924)
"O mio babbino caro"
Leontyne Price
London Symphony Orchestra, Edward Downes

Gianni Schicchi takes place in Florence at the end of the thirteenth century. The wealthy Buoso Donati has died, bequeathing all his money to a group of monks, and his disinherited relatives call upon Gianni Schicchi to correct this unjust situation. Lauretta, Schicchi's daughter, adds her plea because she is in love with one of the disinherited. In the beguiling aria "O mio babbino caro," she threatens to throw herself into the Arno if she cannot marry her chosen fiancé.

Giulio Cesare (Julius Caesar), first performance 1724
George Frideric Handel (1685–1759)
"Non disperar, chi sa?"
Beverly Sills
New York City Opera Orchestra, Julius Rudel

The proud Cleopatra sings of her scorn for her young brother, Ptolemy, her rival to the throne of Egypt. She tells him not to despair for his loss of the kingdom, because he may find a beautiful woman to console him.

Music Notes

I Vespri Siciliani, first performance 1855
Giuseppe Verdi (1813–1901)
"Mercè, dilette amiche"
Montserrat Caballé
Symphonique de Barcelone, G. Masini

On her wedding day to the Sicilian nobleman Arrigo, in 1282, the Hapsburg princess Elena descends a stairway in Palermo. She is presented with flowers by her handmaidens and sings her thanks to them. Her song overflows with the intoxicating joy she feels in anticipation of the great event.

Il Trovatore, first performance 1853
Giuseppe Verdi (1813–1901)
"D'amor sull'ali rosee"
Zinka Milanov
RCA Victor Orchestra, Renato Cellini

In fifteenth-century Spain, the beautiful Leonora sings a prayer for her love to fly over Aliaferia prison's great walls to comfort Manrico, her betrothed, who languishes within. If he cannot be freed, she knows that life will not be worth living.

L'Assedio di Corinto (The Siege of Corinth), first performance 1826
Gioacchino Rossini (1792–1868)
"Giusto ciel! In tal periglio"
Montserrat Caballé
RCA Italiana Opera Orchestra and Chorus, Carlo Felice Cillario

Pamira, daughter of the governor of Corinth at the time of the Ottoman invasion, has unwittingly fallen in love with Maometto, the Turkish sultan, who met her while scouting the city's defenses in disguise. Her father is outraged when the Turk reveals himself and demands not only his surrender but hers as well. In this aria with chorus, Pamira and the women of Corinth raise a last tender plea for heavenly assistance as the hour of their final desperate conflict approaches.

Music Notes

L'Elisir d'Amore, first performance 1832
Gaetano Donizetti (1797–1848)
"Una furtiva lagrima"
Plácido Domingo
London Symphony Orchestra, Nello Santi

Nemorino, the peasant hero of Donizetti's comic opera, is in love with
Adina, daughter of a wealthy landowner, who spurns him. Under the influence
of Dr. Dulcamara's magic elixir, which is really only wine, Nemorino becomes
the center of attention among the young women. Adina, realizing she does love
Nemorino after all, goes sadly away, and he sings of the furtive tear he saw
upon her cheek that revealed her true feelings.

La Bohème, first performance 1896
Giacomo Puccini (1858–1924)
"O soave fanciulla"
Anna Moffo, Richard Tucker
Rome Opera Orchestra, Erich Leinsdorf

In the first act of the world's most-performed opera, Mimi, the poor seamstress, meets the starving poet Rodolfo. He is bold and dashing and, although
she is undeniably drawn to him, she is shy and flustered. At the end of the act,
grasping her tiny cold hand, he declares his love for her with this gorgeous melody.

La Traviata, first performance 1853
Giuseppe Verdi (1813–1901)
"Libiamo, ne' lieti calici"
Anna Moffo, Richard Tucker
Rome Opera Orchestra and Chorus, Fernando Previtali

"Libiamo" is a toast in praise of wine, love, beauty, and the joy of life in
general. Sung first by Alfredo, who is in love with Violetta, the strain is taken
up by the chorus, then by Violetta, who outdoes Alfredo in her expression of
the desire to enjoy life as much as possible for as long as one can.

Music Notes

Les Pêcheurs de Perles (The Pearl Fishers), first performance 1863
Georges Bizet (1838–1875)
"Au fond du temple saint"
Jussi Bjoerling, Robert Merrill
RCA Victor Symphony, Renato Cellini

Nadir and Zurga, two friends in ancient Ceylon, reminisce about a trip they took in their youth to the holy city of Candi. There they saw a beautiful young girl in a crowded temple. So taken were they with her exquisite loveliness that they sing of her as a goddess who had descended among them.

Louise, first performance 1900
Gustave Charpentier (1860–1956)
"Depuis le jour"
Leontyne Price
RCA Italiana Opera Orchestra, Francesco Molinari-Pradelli

Louise, a seamstress living with her parents in their bourgeois apartment, is in love with Julien, a penniless artist. Marriage between the two is forbidden by her parents. To escape the drabness of her life, and because she truly loves Julien, Louise goes to live with him in his Montmartre garret. At the beginning of Act III, as Paris is enveloped in twilight, she sings of her happiness and joy since the day she gave herself to love.

Porgy and Bess, first performance 1935
George Gershwin (1898–1937)
"Summertime"
Leontyne Price
RCA Victor Orchestra, Skitch Henderson

At the beginning of this tale of life and love among the African-Americans of the Charleston waterfront in the 1920s, Clara, a young mother, sings an enchanting lullaby to her baby, who is restless in the heat of the South Carolina summer.

Music Notes

Rigoletto, first performance 1851
Giuseppe Verdi (1813–1901)
"Bella figlia dell'amore" (Quartet)
Anna Moffo, Rosalind Elias, Alfredo Kraus, Robert Merrill
RCA Italiana Opera Orchestra, Georg Solti

First the Duke sings a broad melody in praise of Maddalena, to which she replies with lively banter. Her sparkling phrases are interrupted by interjections from Gilda, and Rigoletto joins in, gloomily asking his daughter to forget her love for the Duke. The four voices are masterfully woven together in a tapestry of sound.

Turandot, first performance 1926
Giacomo Puccini (1858–1924)
"Nessun dorma"
Jussi Bjoerling
Rome Opera Orchestra, Erich Leinsdorf

In legendary Cathay, the Tartar prince Calàf has fallen under the spell of the exquisite Chinese princess Turandot. She has had many suitors put to death for failing to answer her three riddles. Calàf not only answers them, but gives the princess yet another opportunity to triumph if she can guess his true identity before dawn. Turandot decrees that no one in Peking shall sleep until she knows the stranger's name. Alone at night in the royal gardens, Calàf sings that no one shall guess his name until the dawn, when he himself reveals it to Turandot and wins her love.

The headquarters for distinguished chef Larry Forgione, An American Place reflects his philosophy that first-class cooking can be accomplished with exclusively native products. Chef Forgione opened An American Place in 1983 as a formal fifty-seat dining room with a fixed-price menu featuring only American-grown and-produced foods. In 1989, he relocated the restaurant to a larger space in a landmark Art Deco building at Park Avenue and 32nd Street, where he has developed à la carte menus for both lunch and dinner using only American foods.

Regarded as one of America's leading chefs and a catalyst behind new American cuisine, Forgione was named Chef of the Year in 1989 by the Culinary Institute of America, and given the same award in 1993 by the James Beard Awards. One of his food sources is Michigan-based American Spoon Foods, which he co-founded in 1981.

At midday An American Place hums as a setting for business lunches; in the evening the Art Deco–style ceiling lights are dimmed, tables are moved farther apart to allow for more privacy, and the restaurant takes on a more leisurely pace. Selected as one of America's twenty-five best restaurants by Playboy magazine, An American Place has been awarded three stars by the *New York Times*.

The following Harvest Celebration menu illustrates Forgione's signature talent for gracefully updating and refining traditional foods.

THE MENU
An American Place

Roast Corn and Chanterelle Salad with Autumn Greens

*Roast Pheasant with Apple-Sage Dressing, Glazed Onions,
and Roasted-Chestnut Sauce*

Old-fashioned Apple and Cranberry Duff

Serves Six

Roast Corn and Chanterelle Salad with Autumn Greens

5 ears corn on the cob, in the husk
Olive oil for coating, plus 4 tablespoons
12 ounces chanterelle mushrooms, quartered
1 tablespoon minced shallots
1 garlic clove, minced
2 tablespoons cream sherry
2 tablespoons sherry vinegar or cider vinegar
1 teaspoon spicy brown mustard
1 tablespoon minced fresh parsley
1 teaspoon minced fresh rosemary
Salt and freshly ground pepper to taste
4 cups assorted young autumn greens, such as spinach,
    kale, mustard greens, and arugula

Preheat the oven to 350°F. Rinse the ears of corn; pat dry and rub each husk lightly with a little olive oil. Place on a baking sheet and bake in the preheated oven for 15 minutes, turning the ears one or twice. Remove and let cool to room temperature. Pull the husks and all of the corn silk from the ears. With a small, sharp knife, cut the kernels from the cobs and place in a bowl. (You should have about 2½ cups of kernels.)

In a large sauté pan or skillet, heat 2 tablespoons of the olive oil and add the mushrooms. Cook and stir over medium-high heat for 2 minutes. Add the shallots and garlic and cook for 1 minute. Add the sherry and cook over high heat for about 1 minute to reduce by half. Remove the pan from heat and remove the mushrooms with a slotted spoon; add them to the corn.

Pour the liquid from the pan into a small bowl. Whisk in the vinegar, mustard, the remaining 2 tablespoons olive oil, and the herbs to make dressing. Season with salt and pepper. Toss the greens in a bowl with half of the dressing. Spoon onto a platter. Toss the corn and mushrooms with the remaining dressing and spoon over the greens.

Makes 6 servings

An American Place

Roast Pheasant with Apple-Sage Dressing, Glazed Onions, and Roasted-Chestnut Sauce

If you prefer, you may substitute chicken for the pheasant.

½ cup roasted, peeled chestnuts, chopped or
    ⅓ cup (1½ ounces) dried chestnuts
Three 3-pound pheasants
Olive oil for coating, plus 2 tablespoons
Salt and freshly ground black pepper to taste
1 yellow onion, sliced
1 apple, cored and sliced
1 garlic clove, minced

Glazed Onions
3 cups pearl (boiling) onions
1½ cups water
¼ cup sugar
4 tablespoons butter

1½ cups chicken stock (see page 202) or canned low-salt chicken broth
1½ teaspoons cornstarch
½ cup heavy (whipping) cream
2 tablespoons applejack (apple brandy)
Apple-Sage Dressing (recipe follows)
Minced fresh chives for garnish

Place the dried chestnuts in a small saucepan and add water to cover. Cover the pan and simmer over low heat for 1½ to 2 hours, or until the chestnuts are plump. Drain well, chop, and set aside.

Preheat the oven to 375°F. Remove the neck, liver and giblets from the inside of the pheasants. Reserve the livers and giblets for another use. Remove the wings and coarsely chop the wings and necks. Tie the drumsticks securely to the tail with cotton string. Rub the pheasants with olive oil and sprinkle with salt and pepper. Place 2 tablespoons of olive oil in a large roasting pan and place it in the oven for 2 minutes. Place the pheasants one side down in the pan and roast for 15 minutes. Turn onto the other side and roast 15 minutes more.

Remove the pheasants from the oven and spoon off the fat in the pan. Turn the pheasants breast-side up. Add the chopped wings, necks, yellow onion, apple, and garlic to the pan. Roast 30 to 40 minutes more, or until the juices run clear when the thighs are pricked with a fork, stirring the vegetable mixture once or twice. Remove the pheasants from the pan and set aside; keep warm.

Meanwhile, to make the glazed onions: Immerse the pearl onions in boiling water for 3 minutes; drain. Trim off the root ends and gently press to slip off the skins. Place the onions, water, sugar, and butter in a 10-inch skillet. Cook, uncovered, over high heat for 15 to 20 minutes, or until the mixture is golden and onions are caramelized, stirring occasionally. Remove with a slotted spoon, set aside, and keep warm.

To make the sauce, pour off as much fat as possible from the roasting pan. Stir the chicken stock or broth into the pan drippings, scraping up the browned bits on the bottom of the pan. Strain the liquid into a measuring cup and discard any solids. Skim off the fat. Pour the liquid into a medium saucepan and bring to a boil over medium-high heat. Cook uncovered for 8 to 10 minutes, or until reduced to about ½ cup.

In a small bowl, stir together the cornstarch and 1 tablespoon of the cream. Stir the remaining cream into the stock or broth mixture. Add the cornstarch mixture to the stock or broth mixture and cook, stirring, until thickened and bubbly. Reduce heat and cook, stirring, 2 minutes more. Stir in the chestnuts and applejack. Heat through.

Remove the legs and thighs from the pheasants. Discard the legs (they contain a lot of cartilage). Remove the bones from the thighs and cut the breasts away from the bones.

To serve, place a large spoonful of apple-sage dressing in the center of each plate. Arrange a breast and a thigh on each plate. Spoon the sauce over all and surround them with caramelized onions. Sprinkle with the minced chives and serve.

Makes 6 servings

An American Place

Apple-Sage Dressing

This dressing can be made ahead and chilled; bake chilled dressing for about 45 minutes.

2 tablespoons olive oil
2 tablespoons butter
1½ apples, peeled, cored, and cut into ¼-inch cubes (about 1¼ cups)
3 tablespoons minced fresh sage
1 teaspoon minced garlic
⅔ cup finely chopped onion
1¼ cups chicken stock (see page 202) or canned low-salt chicken broth
8 cups cubed dried good-quality bread
¼ teaspoon salt
¼ teaspoon freshly ground black pepper

Preheat the oven to 375°F. In a large sauté pan or skillet, heat the olive oil and 1 tablespoon of the butter over medium heat. Add the apples, sage, garlic, and onion. Cook and stir for 2 minutes. Carefully add the stock or broth and cook 1 minute more.

Place the bread cubes in a large bowl and pour the stock or broth mixture over them; toss to moisten evenly and add the salt and pepper. Place the mixture in a 6-cup casserole. Melt the remaining 1 tablespoon butter and brush it over the dressing. Bake uncovered in the preheated oven for 20 to 25 minutes, or until heated through.

Makes 6 servings

An American Place

Old-fashioned Apple and Cranberry Duff

Fruit

¾ cup sugar

2 tablespoons quick-cooking tapioca

1 cup apple cider

1 cup fresh or frozen cranberries

2 tablespoons applejack (apple brandy)

1 tablespoon grated fresh ginger

Grated zest of 1 lemon

6 red cooking apples such as Macoun or Spy, peeled, cored, and sliced

Topping

2 egg yolks

⅓ cup granulated sugar

1 teaspoon vanilla extract

2 egg whites

¼ cup all-purpose flour

Sifted powdered sugar for garnish

Preheat the oven to 350°F. Butter a 10-cup rectangular baking dish and set it aside.

To prepare the fruit: In a 3-quart saucepan, combine the sugar and tapioca; stir in the apple cider. Cook and stir over medium heat until the sugar is dissolved. Stir in the cranberries, applejack, ginger, and lemon zest. Stir in the sliced apples. Bring to a boil, then reduce heat, cover, and simmer for about 4 minutes, or until the apples are slightly softened. Transfer the mixture to the prepared dish and set aside.

In a medium bowl, beat the egg yolks and granulated sugar until the mixture is thick and pale in color. Stir in the vanilla and set aside. Wash the whisk or beaters. In large bowl, beat the egg whites until soft peaks form. Fold the flour into the beaten whites, then fold this mixture into the yolk mixture and carefully pour the topping over the fruit, spreading it evenly over the surface.

Bake, uncovered, in the preheated oven for 20 to 25 minutes, or until the topping is golden and begins to pull away from the edges of the baking dish. Let cool slightly, sprinkle with powdered sugar, and serve warm.

Makes 6 to 8 servings

An American Place

Bice, short for Beatrice, is named in honor of Beatrice Ruggeri, who founded the original Bice restaurant in Milan in 1926. When Milan became a center for the design and fashion industry, Bice was adopted by the American fashion press. In 1987, at the request of many international patrons, Roberto Ruggeri opened Bice in midtown Manhattan. An instant success, the restaurant managed to transport the ambiance and culinary excellence of the Milanese Bice. Its sleek Art Deco interior, designed by Adam Tihany, opens to the street according to the season, making Bice a charming sidewalk cafe.

Bice's lively dining room offers chef Manuel Mattei's menu of traditional Milanese cuisine and pastry chef Jerry Goldman's luscious desserts. The Ruggeri family has continued to expand their restaurant operations to more than fourteen major cities in the United States and throughout the world.

THE MENU
Bice

Marinated Salmon with Berries and Sambuca

Risotto with Oysters and Black Truffles

John Dory Baked with Potatoes, Porcini Mushrooms, and Rosemary

Chocolate-Hazelnut Tortes with Mocha Zabaione

Serves Four

Marinated Salmon with Berries and Sambuca
Fantasia di Salmone Marinato al Sottobosco e Anice

This beautiful first course of salmon and fresh berries is seasoned with Sambuca, an anise-flavored liqueur.

One 10-ounce salmon fillet
½ cup fresh raspberries
½ cup stemmed fresh strawberries
½ cup fresh blueberries
½ cup fresh blackberries
3 tablespoons dry white wine
1 tablespoon packed brown sugar
1 teaspoon salt
2 tablespoons Sambuca liqueur
1 tablespoon minced fresh dill
Mâche or small lettuce leaves for garnish
Extra-virgin olive oil for drizzling

Slice the salmon fillet lengthwise into thin slices and place the slices on a baking sheet lined with plastic wrap.

Set aside a few of each kind of berry to garnish the plates. In a medium bowl, blend together the remaining berries and wine, saving a few of each kind of berry to garnish the plates. Stir in the brown sugar, salt, and Sambuca. Spread this mixture evenly over the salmon slices. Cover and marinate for 3 hours in the refrigerator.

Remove the salmon slices from the marinade and pat them dry. Divide the slices evenly among 4 plates and sprinkle them lightly with dill. Place some mâche or lettuce leaves in the center of each plate and garnish with the remaining berries. Drizzle with olive oil and serve.

Makes 4 servings

Risotto with Oysters and Black Truffles
Risotto con Ostriche e Tartufo Nero

2 dozen oysters in the shell (Metcalf Bay preferred) or shucked
    fresh oysters in a jar
1 tablespoon olive oil
1 tablespoon minced shallot
1 garlic clove, crushed
1¾ cups Arborio rice
¾ cup champagne
3 cups fish stock (recipe follows), chicken stock (see page 202), or
    canned low-salt chicken broth, heated
1 whole black truffle, julienned
1 tablespoon butter
1 tablespoon minced fresh parsley
Salt and freshly ground white pepper to taste

Shuck the oysters over a bowl or drain the jarred fresh oysters; reserve the oyster liquor. In a heavy saucepan, heat the olive oil over medium heat and sauté the shallot and garlic until very lightly colored, about 5 minutes; remove the garlic clove. Add the rice and cook for 2 minutes. Add ½ cup of the champagne and the reserved oyster liquor, stirring constantly. Cook until this liquid is absorbed. Add the hot stock or broth 1 cup at a time, cooking and stirring each time until the liquid is absorbed, a total of about 12 minutes. Add the truffle to the rice and cook for 4 more minutes. Add the oysters, the remaining ¼ cup champagne, the butter, parsley, and salt and pepper. Remove from heat, cover, and let sit for 2 minutes before serving.

Makes 4 servings

Fish Stock

12 ounces fish bones and scraps, preferably red snapper
1 onion
1 celery stalk
3 fresh thyme sprigs
2 bay leaves
3 parsley sprigs
1 teaspoon white peppercorns
½ cup dry white wine
2 tablespoons salt
8 cups water

Add all the ingredients to a large pot and bring to a boil. Reduce heat to low and simmer for 45 minutes, skimming any foam that rises to the surface. Strain through a fine sieve, pressing the solids with the back of a spoon to extract their juices. Cover and store in the refrigerator for up to 1 week, bringing the stock to a boil every 2 days to keep it from spoiling, or freeze for up to 2 months.

Makes about 8 cups

John Dory Baked with Potatoes, Porcini Mushrooms, and Rosemary
San Pietro al Forno con Patate, Porcini, e Rosmarino

2 Idaho potatoes

4 John Dory, halibut, or turbot fish fillets (1½ pounds)

8 ounces porcini mushrooms, thinly sliced

Leaves from 1 fresh rosemary sprig, minced

¼ cup dry white wine

1 cup cold fish stock (see page 204), chicken stock (see page 202),
   or canned low-salt chicken broth

Salt and freshly ground pepper to taste

1 tablespoon butter

2 tablespoons extra-virgin olive oil

Preheat the oven to 450°F. Butter the bottom of a large baking pan or heat-proof casserole. Peel and thinly slice the potatoes; place them in an overlapping pattern on the bottom of the prepared baking dish or casserole. Place the fish fillets over the potatoes and sprinkle them with the porcini mushrooms and minced rosemary. Add the wine, stock or broth, salt, and pepper. Cover the baking dish or casserole tightly with aluminum foil and bake in the preheated oven for 20 to 25 minutes, or until the fish is opaque throughout.

Remove the fish fillets and arrange one on each of 4 warmed plates. Place the baking pan or casserole over high heat and cook the pan juices until they are reduced to the consistency of syrup. Stir in the butter. Ladle the sauce over the fish, drizzle with extra-virgin olive oil, and serve.

Makes 4 servings

Chocolate-Hazelnut Tortes with Mocha Zabaione
Tortine al Cioccolato e Nicciola con Zabaione di Moka

1 cup peeled hazelnuts (see page 205), ground, plus more for garnish
5 ounces bittersweet or semisweet chocolate, chopped
¾ cup (1½ sticks) butter, cut into pieces
4 eggs, separated
1½ teaspoons flour
3 tablespoons sugar
Mocha Zabaione (recipe follows)
Whipped cream for garnish

Preheat the oven to 450°F. Butter four 3- to 4-inch ring molds and dust them with the ground hazelnuts. Place the molds on a baking sheet lined with parchment paper or aluminum foil. Sprinkle more nuts inside the rings and set aside.

In a double boiler over barely simmering water, melt the chocolate and butter. Stir in the egg yolks and flour and set aside to cool slightly.

In a deep bowl, beat together the egg whites and sugar until soft peaks form. Fold the egg whites into the chocolate mixture and spoon the mixture into the ring molds. Bake in the preheated oven 8 to 10 minutes; the tortes will be slightly underdone in the center.

Let cool to room temperature and remove the molds. Spoon a pool of the zabaione onto each of 4 dessert plates. Invert a torte on top of each pool of sauce. Garnish with whipped cream and more nuts.

Makes four 3- to 4-inch tortes

Mocha Zabaione
Zabaione di Moka

1 cup freshly brewed strong coffee
4 egg yolks
⅓ cup sugar
4 ounces bittersweet or semisweet chocolate, chopped
Rum or Kahlúa to taste

In a double boiler over barely simmering water, whisk together the coffee, egg yolks, and sugar until very thick and hot. Remove from heat. Add the chocolate and stir until it is melted. Place the top of the double boiler in a bowl of ice water, stirring occasionally until cool. Stir in the rum or Kahlúa.

Makes 1½ cups

"When we reopened this venerable restaurant in 1975 it was tempting to fill the menu with dishes associated with operas, singers, and composers, considering the fact that from its 1917 beginning its regulars included just about every musician and artist of note. Lawrence Tibbet even lived in one of the duplex studios of the Hôtel des Artistes, so serving Pêche Melba, the famous dish created for her by Escoffier, or a Fillet of Sole Segovia (another regular at the Café), or a Salad Aida would have been perfectly justified.

"However, after many tastings we felt that instead of this approach we should offer the kind of dishes which these preeminent artists ate on the rare occasions when they could afford the pleasure of eating in their own dining rooms.

"Interestingly, regardless of their nationality, the common culinary denominator was always French regional and home cooking, and the following recipes are a sampling from the Café des Artistes' repertoire."

—George and Jenifer Lang

Café des Artistes

THE MENU

Café des Artistes

Carrot Soup

Breton Scallop Salad

Veal Chops Grand-mère

Languedoc Almond Pie

Serves Six

Carrot Soup
Potage Crécy

4 tablespoons unsalted butter

1½ pounds carrots, peeled and coarsely grated

2 large boiling potatoes, peeled and diced

2 shallots, or 1 small white onion, coarsely chopped

Salt and freshly ground black pepper to taste

Pinch of sugar, or to taste

4 cups veal stock (see page 207), chicken stock (see page 202), or
    canned low-salt chicken broth

Minced fresh flat-leaf (Italian) parsley for garnish

Fresh chervil leaves for garnish

In a heavy 6-quart saucepan, melt the butter over low heat. Add the carrots, potatoes, and shallots or onion, and season with salt, pepper, and sugar. Reduce the heat to very low, cover, and cook for about 15 minutes, stirring often, or until the carrots are very soft, almost a purée. Stir in the stock or broth and simmer uncovered for about 15 minutes more, stirring occasionally.

Remove the pot from the heat. Force the soup, in batches, through the finest blade of a food mill set over a large bowl, until puréed and smooth. Alternatively, purée in batches in a blender or food processor.

Return the soup to the saucepan and place over low heat until warmed through. Adjust the seasoning and garnish with the parsley and chervil. Ladle the warm soup into bowls and serve.

Makes 6 servings

Breton Scallop Salad
Salade de Coquilles St-Jacques Bretonnes

¾ cup olive oil

¼ cup sherry wine vinegar

3 tablespoons minced shallots

Salt and freshly ground pepper to taste

1 cup julienned carrots, blanched until crisp-tender

1 cup julienned green beans, blanched until crisp-tender

1 cup (3 ounces) julienned mushrooms

4 cups water

½ bay leaf

12 large sea scallops

Beurre Blanc for napping (recipe follows)

Finely shredded fresh spinach for garnish

In a small nonaluminum bowl, whisk together the olive oil, vinegar, 2 table-spoons of the shallots, the salt, and pepper until well blended. Add the carrots, green beans, and mushrooms to the vinaigrette and toss gently until well coated; set aside.

In a heavy 6-quart saucepan over high heat, bring the water to a boil. Stir in the remaining 1 tablespoon shallots, bay leaf half, and salt and pepper to taste. Reduce heat to medium and simmer for 10 minutes. Add the scallops and poach until they are opaque and slightly firm but still springy to the touch, about 1 minute. Remove from heat and drain, discarding the bay leaf half.

Divide the salad among 6 plates and mound the salad in the center of the plate. Slice 2 poached scallops crosswise into thin rounds and arrange in a slightly overlapping circle around the salad. Nap the scallops with beurre blanc and surround with shredded spinach. Serve immediately.

Makes 6 servings

Café des Artistes

Beurre Blanc

1 teaspoon minced shallot
3 tablespoons dry white wine
2 teaspoons fresh lemon juice
1 cup heavy (whipping) cream at room temperature
½ pound (2 sticks) unsalted butter, chilled and cut into 20 pieces
Salt and freshly ground black pepper to taste

In a large nonaluminum saucepan, combine the shallot, wine, and lemon juice, and boil until almost evaporated.

Whisk in the cream and boil, beating constantly, until the mixture begins to thicken. Keeping the mixture at a boil, beat in 1 piece of butter at a time until all the butter is incorporated. (The sauce should now be thickened.) Season to taste with salt and white pepper and serve at once, or keep warm over a bowl of barely tepid water.

Makes about 2 cups

Café des Artistes

Veal Chops Grand-mère

7½ tablespoons unsalted butter
Six 6-ounce veal chops, about 1 inch thick, trimmed
6 ounces slab bacon, blanched and cut into ¼-inch dice
6 ounces mushrooms, sliced or whole
8 small white boiling onions
12 unpeeled small new potatoes
1½ cups dry white wine
6 tablespoons chicken stock (see page 202) or canned low-salt chicken broth
Salt and freshly ground pepper to taste

In a large, heavy sauté pan or skillet, melt 4½ tablespoons of the butter over medium heat. Add the veal chops and sauté for about 10 minutes on each side, or until lightly browned on the outside but slightly pink in the center. Remove from heat and set the skillet with the chops aside.

In a small, heavy skillet, melt 1½ tablespoons of the butter and fry the bacon for about 4 minutes, or until evenly browned and crisp. Add the mushrooms and sauté for a few minutes, or until golden brown. Carefully pour off the excess fat, remove the skillet from heat, and set aside.

To a 3-quart saucepan of boiling salted water, add the onions and potatoes and boil until tender, about 20 minutes. Drain the vegetables and peel the potatoes. Set aside.

Transfer the veal chops to a casserole. Add the bacon mixture, onions, and potatoes. Return the veal chop skillet to high heat and add the wine; bring to a boil and cook for 1 minute, stirring to scrape up the browned bits from the bottom and sides of the skillet. Add this liquid, along with the stock or broth, to the casserole. Season with salt and pepper, stir in the remaining 1½ tablespoons of the butter, and serve.

Makes 6 servings

Café des Artistes

Languedoc Almond Pie

If you don't have time to make your own puff pastry, use thawed frozen puff pastry.

Puff Pastry Crust
3 cups sifted all-purpose flour
1 teaspoon salt
2 large egg yolks
4 tablespoons unsalted butter, chilled and finely chopped, plus ¾ cup
    (1½ sticks) unsalted butter, chilled and cut into small dice
1 tablespoon milk, plus more if needed

Filling
⅔ cup (3 ounces) ground blanched almonds
1 tablespoon orange flower water (available at some supermarkets and
    specialty foods stores)
1 teaspoon grated orange zest
1 teaspoon grated lemon zest
1 large egg yolk, lightly beaten
Thinly sliced candied angelica stem for garnish (available at bakery
    supply stores and specialty foods stores)
Sifted confectioners' sugar for dusting

To prepare the puff pastry crust: Place the flour in a mound on a work surface and make a well in the center of the flour. Place the salt, egg yolks, and the 4 tablespoons finely chopped butter in the center of the well. Working quickly and using your fingers, lightly work the mixture together with the milk. Add enough milk to allow the dough to just hold together.

Gather the dough into a loose ball and place it on a lightly floured work surface. Using the heel of your hand, push the dough away from you just until the butter has been smeared and incorporated into the dough. Form the dough into a ball, cover with plastic wrap, and refrigerate for 30 minutes.

In a small bowl, place the ¾ cup diced butter and work the butter with a wooden spoon until it has the same consistency as the pastry and is cold and pliable but not soft.

Place the dough on a lightly floured work surface, roll out the dough, and place the butter in a flat mound in the center of the dough. Fold the pastry over the butter, covering it completely. Using a rolling pin, lightly hit the dough-covered butter mound to flatten it to about a ¼-inch thickness.

Roll the dough out to a 14-by-7-inch rectangle. Fold down the top third of the dough and fold the bottom third up to meet it so that the edges meet in the center. (The dough will be crumbly, but it will become smoother as you work it.) Fold one half of the dough over the other to form a 7-by-3½-inch rectangle. Using a rolling pin, lightly pound the rectangle to seal the fold. This is the first fold. Cover with plastic wrap and refrigerate for 10 minutes.

Rotate the pastry so the folded edge is on your right and repeat the rolling and folding steps in the preceding paragraph; this is the second fold. (To keep track of the folds, use your knuckle to make a light impression in the dough twice to mark 2 folds.) Cover with plastic wrap and refrigerate for 10 minutes.

Repeat the rolling and folding steps 3 more times and return the pastry to the refrigerator for 10 minutes after each of the 3 folds. You should now have a total of 5 impressions in the dough for the 5 folds. Form the dough into 2 flat disks, wrap in plastic wrap, and refrigerate until ready to use.

To prepare the filling: Preheat the oven to 375°F. In a medium nonaluminum bowl, combine the almonds, orange flower water, orange zest, and lemon zest, and stir until well blended; set aside.

On a lightly floured work surface, roll out the balls of dough ¼ inch thick. Trim to two 10-inch circles. Lightly moisten the edge of an 8-inch pie pan with water and fit the bottom crust into the pan.

Fill the pie with the filling. Lightly moisten the edge of the pastry and carefully place the top crust on top of the filling. Crimp the edges to seal. Lightly brush

Café des Artistes

the crust with the beaten egg yolk and cut vents into the surface with the sharp point of a knife.

Bake in the preheated oven for 40 minutes, or until the crust is golden brown. Dust with confectioners' sugar and decorate with the angelica. Serve at room temperature.

Makes 6 to 8 servings

Chanterelle

People choose to dine at Chanterelle for the sheer love of good food. Chef David Waltuck is a culinary artist whose imaginative adaptation of classic French cuisine has earned his restaurant four stars from the *New York Times.* A graduate of the Culinary Institute of America, chef Waltuck has created a superb restaurant and remained true to himself. Karen Waltuck, the maîtresse d'hôtel, sets the tone for the restaurant's elegant, flawless service.

Diners may choose from a specially created menu that includes three full courses at lunch or six smaller courses at dinner. There is also a selection of à la carte offerings at lunch and a fixed-price three-course evening meal.

Chanterelle is located in a building that was once New York's Mercantile Exchange Building in TriBeCa, a neighborhood that has been converted from industrial to mostly residential use by artists in search of affordable studio space. Menu covers for Chanterelle have been designed by such artistic friends of the house as John Cage, Virgil Thomson, and Marcel Marceau. The spare but lovely dining room has an ornate stamped tin ceiling, gorgeous flowers, and soft lighting. The restaurant's excellent wine list offers something in almost every price range.

Chanterelle

THE MENU
Chanterelle

Terrine of Smoked Salmon and Caviar

Melon Soup with Summer Fruit

Scallops with Tomato and Thyme

Beef with Black Trumpet Mushrooms

Raspberry Gratin

Serves Eight

Terrine of Smoked Salmon and Caviar

Begin this recipe one day before you plan to serve the terrine.

14 ounces smoked Norwegian salmon
6 ounces clarified unsalted butter (see page 202)
¼ cup heavy (whipping) cream, preferably not ultrapasteurized
1½ teaspoons fresh lemon juice or more to taste
Pinch each of minced fresh chives, dill, and parsley
3 ounces black caviar
Cucumber Salad (recipe follows)
Lemon wedges and toast for serving

Thinly slice 6 ounces of the salmon and set aside. Chop the remaining salmon into ½-inch cubes. In a blender or food processor, purée the salmon cubes, clarified butter, and cream in batches, if necessary, until completely smooth and fluffy. Stir in the lemon juice, chives, dill, and parsley. Adjust the seasoning by adding a bit more lemon, if necessary. Salt need not be added since the remaining ingredients are salty. Set the mousse aside.

To assemble, line a 2-cup terrine mold with a piece of parchment paper or aluminum foil large enough to overhang the edges and fold over the top of the terrine. Cover the bottom of the terrine with a layer of sliced salmon. Using a metal spatula, spread a thin layer of salmon mousse on top of the salmon slices. Top the salmon mousse with a thin layer of black caviar. Repeat these layers until the terrine is full. Top with the remaining sliced salmon. Fold the paper or foil over the top of the terrine. Chill in the refrigerator for 24 hours.

Unmold the terrine by dipping it very briefly in a bowl of hot water. Unfold the paper or foil at the end of the terrine. Turn the terrine over and gently pull at the end of the paper or foil to release the terrine. Cover with plastic wrap and chill again in the refrigerator for 30 minutes.

To serve, slice the terrine thinly with a knife that has been dipped in hot water. Serve with cucumber salad, lemon wedges, and toast.

Makes 8 to 10 servings

Cucumber Salad

2 medium cucumbers
½ cup crème fraîche (see page 203)
2 teaspoons fresh lemon juice
1 tablespoon minced fresh dill
Salt and freshly ground pepper to taste

Peel the cucumbers, cut them in half lengthwise, remove the seeds, and slice thinly. In a large bowl, toss together the cucumber slices and all the remaining ingredients. Cover with plastic wrap and refrigerate until chilled.

Makes about 3 cups

Chanterelle

Melon Soup with Summer Fruit

2 ripe honeydew melons, or 4 cantaloupes or cavaillon melons
½ cup superfine sugar, or to taste
1 cup Muscat, Beaune de Venice, Vin Santo, or Sauternes wine
4 blood oranges, peeled, seeded, and sliced crosswise
½ pineapple, cut into 1-inch-thick slices
12 fresh strawberries, stemmed and sliced
32 fresh blackberries
4 handfuls fresh blueberries
2 handfuls fresh raspberries
1 pink grapefruit, cut into sections (see page 206)
4 fresh mint sprigs or unsprayed edible mild-tasting flowers
    such as pansies or rose petals for garnish

Scoop the pulp out of the melons and purée it in a blender or food processor. Stir in the sugar until it completely dissolves. Add more sugar to taste, if
necessary. Stir in the wine. Cover and refrigerate until the mixture is chilled.

Divide the orange slices, pineapple slices, strawberries, blackberries, blueberries, raspberries, and grapefruit sections among 8 shallow soup bowls, arranging the fruit in a pretty pattern. Ladle the soup over the fruit and garnish with mint
sprigs or flowers.

Makes 8 servings

Scallops with Tomato and Thyme

Blanched thin asparagus or green beans are a pretty garnish because their shape allows them to be arranged between the scallops.

2 cups dry white wine
3 tablespoons minced shallots
2 cups chicken stock (see page 202) or canned low-salt chicken broth
2 cups fish stock (see page 204), chicken stock (see page 202),
    or canned low-salt chicken broth
1 cup chopped fresh or canned tomatoes
Soybean oil for sautéing
3 pounds sea scallops, rinsed and patted dry with paper towels
6 tablespoons tomato concassée (see page 206)
Pinch of minced fresh thyme
2 tablespoons virgin olive oil
1 squeeze fresh lemon juice
Salt and freshly ground pepper to taste
Seasonal vegetables for garnish

To a large saucepan or stockpot, add the white wine, shallots, chicken stock or broth, fish or chicken stock or broth, and chopped tomatoes; bring to a boil and cook to reduce the liquid by a third. Strain through a fine-meshed sieve and set aside.

Film the bottom of a large skillet or sauté pan with soybean oil and heat until very hot. Sauté the scallops, in batches, for about 2 minutes on each side, or until well browned but still translucent at the center. Remove the scallops from the pan and add the wine sauce. Bring to a boil, stirring to scrape up the browned juices on the bottom of the pan, and cook to reduce the liquid by half. Stir in the tomato concassée, thyme, olive oil, lemon juice, and salt and pepper.

Divide the sauce among 8 plates and arrange the scallops on top. Garnish with seasonal vegetables and serve.

Makes 8 servings

Beef with Black Trumpet Mushrooms

2 tablespoons unsalted butter
1 pound black trumpet mushrooms or chanterelles, sliced
Olive oil for browning
3 pounds beef tenderloin
3 tablespoons brandy
1½ tablespoons beef or veal glaze (see page 201)
1 tablespoon fresh lemon juice
¾ cup heavy (whipping) cream
Salt and freshly ground pepper to taste
Seasonal vegetables for garnish

Preheat the oven to 400°F. In a large sauté pan or skillet, melt 1 tablespoon of the butter over medium heat and sauté the mushrooms. When they begin to give off some liquid, drain them, reserving the liquid and the mushrooms.

Film a large sauté pan or skillet with olive oil and cook the beef over high heat until nicely browned. Place the beef in the preheated oven and bake for 10 minutes, or until rare. Remove from the oven and cover to keep warm.

In a medium sauté pan or skillet, melt the remaining 1 tablespoon of butter over medium heat and cook the sautéed mushrooms until dry and slightly crisp. Remove the pan from heat and add the brandy. Return the pan to heat and let the brandy warm. Ignite the brandy with a match and shake the pan until the flames have subsided. Add the reserved mushroom liquid, the beef or veal glaze, and 1 ½ teaspoons of the lemon juice. Bring to a boil, add the cream, and cook to reduce until thick enough to coat the back of a spoon. Season with salt, pepper, and additional lemon juice, if necessary. Add any juices that may have accumulated on the platter on which the beef was resting.

Divide the sauce and mushrooms evenly among 4 plates. Slice the beef tenderloin and place the slices on top of the sauce and mushrooms. Garnish with seasonal vegetables and serve.

Makes 8 servings

Chanterelle

Raspberry Gratin

6 egg yolks
1 cup Muscat wine
½ cup sugar
1 cup whipped cream
2 cups raspberry coulis (see page 205)
5 cups fresh raspberries

To prepare the sabayon: In a double boiler over barely simmering water, combine the egg yolks, Muscat, and sugar; whisk until foamy and very hot. Remove from heat and place the top of the double boiler in a bowl of ice water; whisk occasionally until completely cooled. Fold in the whipped cream.

To assemble the gratin: Preheat the broiler. Divide the raspberry coulis among 8 shallow porcelain ramekins or other individual ovenproof containers. Add a dollop of sabayon mixture on top. Place an equal amount of fresh raspberries in each dollop of sabayon. Place under the preheated broiler for 2 to 3 minutes, or until lightly browned. Serve warm.

Makes 8 servings

Felice and Lidia Bastianich opened their popular Italian restaurant in 1981. Lidia Bastianich, the inspiration and guiding spirit behind the restaurant, is the author of a cookbook on the foods of her native Istria, a food historian, and active in the Ordine Ristoratori Professionisti Italiani. She creates dishes that are translated into Felidia favorites by chef Mauro Mafrici. The menu highlights the foods of Northern Italy and combines home cooking with the stylish presentation of *nuova cucina.*

Felidia has been awarded three stars by the *New York Times* and voted the Best Italian Restaurant in America by *Playboy* magazine. Dinners are served here in rustic and inviting rooms with exposed-brick walls, Tuscan tiles, and open wine racks. The restaurant's extensive wine list is especially strong in Barolos and Barbarescos. Upstairs, a wood-paneled private dining room can accommodate up to forty-five people.

Felidia Ristorante

THE MENU
Felidia Ristorante

Asparagus Salad

Lobster Stew

Roast Chicken with Pomegranate

Molded Ice Cream with Almonds

Serves Four

Asparagus Salad
Insalata di Asparagi

2 pounds asparagus, trimmed and peeled
2 hard-cooked eggs
3 tablespoons wine vinegar
4 tablespoons olive oil
½ teaspoon salt
Freshly ground black pepper to taste

In a large nonaluminum pot of boiling salted water, cook the asparagus until crisp-tender, about 6 minutes. Drain immediately and rinse under cold running water. Pat the asparagus dry with paper towels and cut into ½-inch pieces. Coarsely chop the cooked egg whites and yolks.

In a large bowl, whisk together the vinegar, oil, salt, and pepper. Add the asparagus pieces and toss well. Add the egg whites and yolks and stir to combine thoroughly.

Makes 4 servings

Felidia Ristorante

Lobster Stew
Aragosta in Brodetto

4 small rock (Pacific) lobsters
Flour for dredging
3 tablespoons vegetable oil
6 tablespoons olive oil
3 onions, diced (about 2 cups)
4 tablespoons tomato paste
⅓ cup red wine vinegar
4 cups hot water
¼ to ½ teaspoon salt
3 cups crushed Roma (plum) tomatoes
Dried red pepper flakes (optional)

Cut off the lobster tails at the body junctures. Dredge the exposed lobster tail meat lightly in flour, shaking off the excess. In a large sauté pan or skillet, heat the vegetable oil over very high heat almost to the smoking point and add the lobster tails meat-side down. Sauté until golden brown, about 2 minutes. Remove the tails from the pan and set aside.

In a large nonaluminum saucepan or stockpot, heat 4 tablespoons of the olive oil and sauté the onions over medium heat until they are translucent, 3 to 4 minutes. Add the lobster bodies and sauté for 5 minutes. Stir in the tomato paste and cook for an additional 5 minutes. Blend the vinegar with the hot water and add it to the pan, raise the heat to high, and bring to a full boil. Add the salt and tomatoes, and boil for 3 minutes.

Remove the lobster bodies with tongs, allowing all the interior juices to drain back into the sauce. (The bodies should be reserved for other uses or, if the meal is to be informal, they may be served on a communal platter in the center of the table. The most delicate meat is in the bodies and should not be wasted.) Add the lobster claws to the sauce and cook for 7 minutes. Add the reserved tails and the remaining olive oil. (If the lobster stew is being served with capellini or spaghetti, the pasta should be added to the boiling water at this point.) Cook the stew 3 to 5 minutes longer over high heat, skimming off any foam that rises to the surface. Remove the tails and claws from the stew and cover to keep warm. Boil the sauce briefly to reduce and concentrate the flavors. Add the hot pepper flakes, if desired.

To serve with capellini or spaghetti, toss the drained pasta with half of the sauce. Flank the pasta with lobster pieces and spoon over the remaining sauce. Otherwise, divide the lobster pieces among 4 plates and ladle the sauce over.

Makes 4 servings

Felidia Ristorante

Roast Chicken with Pomegranate
Pollo Arrosto al Melograno

Two 2-pound chickens, split in half
¼ teaspoon salt
¼ teaspoon freshly ground black pepper
3 tablespoons olive oil
2 large pomegranates
2 tablespoons fresh rosemary leaves
6 tablespoons Grand Marnier
2 tablespoons brandy
2 tablespoons butter
¼ cup chicken stock (see page 202) or canned low-salt chicken broth

Preheat the oven to 500°F. Cut the backbones from the chicken halves and remove the breastbones and ribs. Season the chicken with salt and pepper inside and out.

In 2 very large dry ovenproof skillets, brown the chickens, skin-side down, over high heat for 5 minutes. Turn the chickens over and brown 5 minutes longer. Add the olive oil, transfer the skillets to the preheated oven, and bake, turning the chickens occasionally, for 30 minutes, or until the juices run clear when the thighs are pricked with a fork.

Meanwhile, cut the pomegranates in half and juice them with an orange juicer; take care, as pomegranate juice stains. Set the juice aside (you should have at least ½ cup).

When the chickens are done, remove the skillets from the oven and drain off all the fat from the pans. Add the rosemary and Grand Marnier, ¼ cup of the pomegranate juice and half of the brandy, the butter, and chicken stock or broth to each pan. Place the skillets over high heat and cook for 2 minutes while basting and turning the chickens. Transfer the chickens to 4 plates and spoon the sauce over.

Makes 4 servings

Felidia Ristorante

Molded Ice Cream with Almonds
Semifreddo alle Mandorle

½ cup (2 ounces) whole almonds
4 ounces semisweet chocolate, grated
6 amaretti cookies, crumbled
1 tablespoon brandy
5 eggs, separated
1 cup superfine sugar
2 cups heavy (whipping) cream

Preheat the broiler. Spread the almonds on a baking sheet, place it a few inches from the heat of the broiler, and turn the almonds until golden, about 2 minutes. Remove from heat immediately, let cool, and finely chop; set aside. In a small bowl, stir together the chocolate, amaretti crumbs, and brandy; set aside.

In a deep bowl, beat the egg whites until foamy. Gradually add ½ cup of the sugar while beating until stiff peaks form. In a large bowl, beat the egg yolks with the remaining sugar until the mixture is thick and pale in color. In a deep bowl, whip the cream until stiff peaks form. Gently fold together the whites into the yolks, then gently fold in the whipped cream.

Line a 9-inch loaf pan with plastic wrap. Spoon one third of the egg mixture into the pan and tap the bottom of the pan on a hard surface to settle the mixture. Sprinkle half of the chocolate mixture over the surface in an even layer. Repeat, finishing with the last third of the egg mixture. Smooth the surface with a spatula, cover with plastic wrap, and freeze overnight.

To serve, invert the pan and tap the bottom sharply to loosen the frozen mixture. Remove the plastic wrap and cut the ice cream into ¾-inch-thick slices. The dessert will keep in plastic wrap for about 1 week in the freezer.

Makes 6 to 8 servings

THE FOUR SEASONS

Since The Four Seasons opened its doors in 1959, men and women from every frontier of culture, the leaders of our creative society, have gathered to dine in its elegant contemporary setting. Owners Paul Kovi and Tom Margittai are committed to change and creativity, and their restaurant is a constantly evolving experience that reflects the vitality of New York. Each spring, summer, fall, and winter new menus are created to explore the abundance and variety of the season. New dishes appear daily, and significant changes, such as the development of the restaurant's popular Spa Cuisine, are always being made in response to the public's desire to dine wisely and well. Executive chef Christian "Hitsch" Albin endeavors to bring a new spirit to classical cuisine and "make food with a lot of flavor, a lot of herbs, food that looks light, tastes light, but is powerful." The restaurant's renowned wine cellar is especially strong in California, Italian, and Bordeaux selections.

Located in the Seagrams Building on Park Avenue, The Four Seasons restaurant was designed by Philip Johnson and was designated an architectural landmark by the New York Landmarks Commission. The two large square rooms are framed by wood paneling and walls of windows with rippling chain draperies. A huge Picasso tapestry, a 1929 stage backdrop for Diaghilev's *Le Tricorne,* hangs in the corridor connecting the two rooms. The Pool Room, with its graciously appointed tables, illuminated trees, and a gurgling marble pool is a serene setting for luxurious dining. The slightly less formal Grill Room, with its Richard Lippold sculpture of brass rods hanging from the ceiling over the bar, is host at midday to its prominent regulars and in the evening to a younger audience eager for reasonable fixed-price dinners and a specially chosen list of affordable American wines.

The Four Seasons

THE MENU
The Four Seasons

Smoked Salmon Roulades

Risotto with Oyster Mushrooms, Morels, and Asparagus

Baked Turbot with Tomato

Raspberry Summer Pudding

Serves Four

Smoked Salmon Roulades

1 bunch fresh chives
½ medium cucumber, cut into ¼-inch-thick slices
4 small radishes, trimmed
10 ounces smoked salmon, thinly sliced
1 small celery root, about 12 ounces
1 teaspoon wasabi powder (available in Asian markets)
2 teaspoons water
6 tablespoons sour cream
4 ounces black caviar

Bring a medium saucepan of water to boil. Select 10 long chives from the bunch and plunge them into the boiling water. (Reserve the remaining chives for garnish.) Bring the water back to a boil, drain, and rinse the chives under cold running water. Dry on paper towels. Place the cucumber slices and radishes in ice water to crisp.

Place the salmon slices on a large work surface and cut them into uniform rectangles. (Finely chop the trimmings and reserve for the stuffing.) Peel the celery root and cut it into a very fine dice. In a small bowl, dissolve the wasabi powder in the water.

In a small bowl, combine the celery root, sour cream, dissolved wasabi, and reserved smoked salmon trimmings. Mix well. Divide the stuffing between the rectangles of salmon and spread evenly with the back of a spoon. Roll the salmon into compact cylinders. Use the blanched chives as "strings" to secure the roulades. Trim off the ends. Serve on a large platter and garnish with the remaining chives, the rounds of cucumber, radishes, and caviar.

Makes 4 servings

The Four Seasons

Risotto with Oyster Mushrooms, Morels, and Asparagus

10 asparagus spears

6 cups chicken stock (see page 202) or canned low-salt chicken broth, heated

10 tablespoons plus 4 teaspoons extra-virgin olive oil

10 or 12 morels (6 ounces), sliced crosswise

4 shallots, minced

2 cups (6 ounces) oyster mushrooms, stemmed

Kosher salt and freshly ground black pepper to taste

2 cups Arborio rice

½ cup dry white wine

2 garlic cloves, minced

2 tablespoons unsalted butter

1 jalapeño chili, seeded and finely chopped

½ cup minced fresh flat-leaf (Italian) parsley

1 heaping tablespoon grated Parmesan cheese

Peel the asparagus spears and trim 1 inch from the ends. In a saucepan, simmer the asparagus ends in the chicken stock or broth for 30 minutes; set aside.

Bring a large pot of salted water to a boil and cook the asparagus spears for 2 to 3 minutes, or until crisp-tender. Drain and chop into ¼-inch-thick slices, saving the tips for garnish; set aside.

In a saucepan over high heat, heat 4 tablespoons of the olive oil and sauté the morels. Add half the shallots and sauté for about 2 minutes. Add the oyster mushrooms and sauté for 2 to 3 minutes. Season with kosher salt and a pinch of pepper; set aside.

In a medium saucepan, heat 6 tablespoons of the olive oil over medium heat and sauté the remaining chopped shallots until translucent, about 3 minutes. Add the rice to the pan and stir until it is opaque. Add the wine, garlic, kosher salt to taste, and ½ cup stock or broth, and stir until the stock or broth is absorbed. Continue pouring in the stock or broth in ½-cup increments and stirring until all of it has been absorbed, about 15 minutes.

In a medium saucepan over low heat, combine the remaining 4 teaspoons olive oil, butter, risotto, jalapeño, and salt to taste. Add the oyster mushrooms, morels, and shallots and stir until heated through. Add the parsley and asparagus slices last or the vegetables will lose their flavor. Add the Parmesan cheese and remove from heat immediately.

Serve the risotto in shallow soup bowls, leveling the mound on each plate with a wooden spoon. Garnish with the asparagus tips.

Makes 4 servings

Baked Turbot with Tomato

Sauce

¼ cup dry white wine

2 tablespoons minced shallots

2 tablespoons white wine vinegar

1 cup heavy (whipping) cream

3 tablespoons unsalted butter, chilled and cut into small pieces

Salt and freshly ground pepper to taste

2 teaspoons Dijon mustard

1 tablespoon Pommery mustard

Fish

4 turbot fillets, about 6 ounces each

Salt and freshly ground pepper to taste

2 tablespoons unsalted butter

4 large tomatoes, cored, peeled, and quartered

2 tablespoons Pommery mustard

2 teaspoons minced fresh thyme, or 1 teaspoon dried thyme

3 tablespoons extra-virgin olive oil

Garnish

1 tablespoon unsalted butter

8 ounces snow peas, blanched

Salt and freshly ground pepper to taste

8 fresh thyme sprigs

To make the sauce: In a small, heavy saucepan, combine the wine, shallots, and vinegar. Cook over high heat until reduced by half. Reduce the heat to low. Add the cream and cook again to reduce by half. Moving the pan on and off heat to regulate the melting, whisk in the butter, 1 piece at a time, until the sauce is thick and emulsified. Add salt and pepper. Strain through a fine-meshed sieve into a heatproof bowl. Stir in the mustards and keep warm over a pan of barely simmering water until ready to serve.

To prepare the fish: Preheat the oven to 375°F. Season the turbot with salt and pepper. In a medium, heavy sauté pan or skillet, melt the butter over high heat. Add the fish and cook just enough to sear both sides, about 30 seconds on each side. Transfer to a platter and let cool completely.

Remove the seeds from the quartered tomatoes. Cut each quarter into 4 equal pieces. Spread the mustard on one side of each of the fish fillets and sprinkle with thyme. Place the tomato pieces side by side in rows on top of each fillet to completely cover the fish. Drizzle the olive oil over. Place the fish in a lightly oiled baking dish and sprinkle it with a few drops of water to prevent the fish from sticking to the dish. Bake for 5 minutes, or just until firm to the touch.

Meanwhile, to prepare the garnish: In a large skillet or sauté pan, melt the butter over medium-high heat. Add the peas, season with salt and pepper, and sauté, stirring often, until the peas are heated through, 2 to 3 minutes.

Spoon a small amount of the sauce over the bottom of each of 4 warmed serving plates. Place a turbot fillet with tomato topping in the center of each plate. Arrange the snow peas on the top part of each plate and garnish with 2 thyme sprigs. Serve at once.

Make 4 servings

Raspberry Summer Pudding

12 cups fresh raspberries

¾ cup sugar

1 pound white bread, sliced and crusts removed

2 tablespoons raspberry jam or preserves, melted with 1 tablespoon water

Garnish

¼ cup heavy (whipping) cream, or ½ cup crème fraîche (see page 203)

4 fresh mint leaves

Candied violets (optional)

Lightly rinse 8 cups of the raspberries. Place them in a large bowl with the sugar and mix with a wooden spatula until the berries are just crushed. Macerate the berries, stirring them occasionally, for about 1 hour, or until they are half liquefied. (The sugar will draw the juice out of the berries.)

Line the bottom of a round 6-by-2-inch cake pan with a sheet of plastic wrap, leaving enough to cover the top of the pudding later on. Neatly spoon a very thin layer of berries (just enough to coat) over the bottom of the pan. Top with a layer of bread fitted together neatly like the pieces of a puzzle. Continue layering until you have 3 layers of bread alternating with 4 layers of raspberries. All the layers of raspberries, except the bottom layer, should be the same thickness as the bread. (There may be a little raspberry-sugar mixture left over.) Cover the top of the cake with the reserved plastic wrap, then place a weight on top. Refrigerate overnight.

Knock the pan on a table to loosen the pudding, then unmold it carefully onto a 6-inch round piece of cardboard or a cake plate. Remove the plastic wrap.

Lightly rinse the remaining 4 cups berries and dry them on paper towels. Mix the melted raspberry jam or preserves with the berries, taking care not to bruise them. Cover the top of the pudding with the berries, arranging them in concentric circles.

To serve, slice generously and garnish with whipped cream or crème fraîche, mint leaves, and the optional candied violets.

Makes 6 servings

IL CANTINORI

Il Cantinori, which serves the robust fare of Italy's Tuscany region, has had a marked impact on Italian cooking in America since it was opened in 1983 by proprietors Frank Minieri, Steve Tzolis, and Nicola Kotsoni. The popular flower-filled Greenwich Village restaurant has a romantic Tuscan country-house setting. White stucco walls, terra-cotta flooring, and wood-beamed ceilings enhance the lively dining rooms, and a terrace provides outdoor dining when the weather permits. Chef Antonio Cinardi's menu changes weekly, and a host of specials are offered daily.

THE MENU
Il Cantinori

Spaghetti with Broccoli Rabe and Radicchio

Mixed Mushrooms with Arugula

Braised Baby Octopus with Garlic Toast

Pumpkin-Polenta Cookies

Serves Eight

Spaghetti with Broccoli Rabe and Radicchio
Spaghetti con Broccoli Rabe e Radicchio

Broccoli rabe, also called rapini, is a green vegetable with leafy stalks that resemble sprouting broccoli. Its peppery flavor complements the slightly bitter taste of radicchio in this dish.

¼ cup olive oil
1 head radicchio, leaves separated and cut into shreds
Salt and freshly ground pepper to taste
1 pound spaghetti
4 garlic cloves, peeled and chopped
2 pounds broccoli rabe, cut into 2-inch pieces
½ teaspoon dried red pepper flakes
Olive oil for sprinkling

Preheat the oven to 350°F. Film the bottom of a shallow baking dish with olive oil, add the radicchio, and sprinkle with salt and pepper. Bake until the radicchio is lightly browned. Set aside.

In a large pot of boiling, salted water, cook the spaghetti at a rolling boil for 10 to 12 minutes, or until al dente. Drain, reserving a little of the cooking water.

Meanwhile, in a large sauté pan or skillet, heat 2 tablespoons of the olive oil over medium-high heat and sauté the garlic until lightly browned, about 4 minutes. Add the broccoli rabe, red pepper, and salt to taste, and sauté until the broccoli rabe is crisp-tender, about 5 minutes. Add the browned radicchio and mix thoroughly. Add the drained spaghetti to the pan with a few table-spoonfuls of the cooking water; mix well. Sprinkle with olive oil and serve at once.

Makes 8 servings

Il Cantinori

Mixed Mushrooms with Arugula
Funghi Misti con Rugola

4 bunches arugula
¼ cup olive oil
3 garlic cloves, chopped
1 pound (4 cups) shiitake mushrooms, stemmed and sliced
1 pound (4 cups) oyster mushrooms, sliced
Salt and freshly ground pepper to taste
2 tablespoons balsamic vinegar, plus more for sprinkling
Olive oil for sprinkling

Trim the arugula, discarding the stems (you should have about 8 cups of leaves); rinse and dry well. In a large sauté pan or skillet heat the olive oil over medium-high heat, and sauté the garlic until it has colored lightly, about 4 minutes. Add the mushrooms and sauté for about 5 minutes, draining off any excess water. Remove from heat and season with salt, pepper, and the 2 tablespoons of balsamic vinegar.

Transfer the arugula to a large serving bowl. Sprinkle with balsamic vinegar and olive oil to taste and toss. Top with the sautéed mushrooms and serve.

Makes 8 servings

Braised Baby Octopus with Garlic Toast
Polpetti in Umido con Bruschetta

This recipe calls for tiny octopus weighing no more than 10 ounces each.

2 pounds baby octopus, cleaned
½ cup extra-virgin olive oil
1½ garlic cloves, minced
Salt, freshly ground black pepper, and dried red pepper flakes to taste
1½ cups dry white wine
6 ripe tomatoes (4½ pounds), peeled and seeded, or 3 cups canned tomatoes
8 slices garlic toast (see page 204)
1 tablespoon minced fresh parsley

Separate the tentacles from the body of each baby octopus and peel the skin away from the head. In a large saucepan, heat the olive oil over medium heat and sauté the garlic until golden brown, about 5 minutes. Add the octopus to the pan and cook for about 5 minutes, or until it turns color. Add the salt, black pepper, and red pepper flakes, and toss. Add the wine and simmer for about 10 minutes.

Meanwhile, purée the tomatoes in a blender or food processor. Add the purée to the pan with the octopus and simmer for 10 to 15 minutes, or until the octopus is tender and the sauce has thickened a little. Spoon over garlic toasts and sprinkle with parsley.

Makes 8 servings

Pumpkin-Polenta Cookies
Biscotti di Zucca e Polenta

½ cup shelled pumpkin seeds

½ cup (1 stick) unsalted butter at room temperature

6 tablespoons sugar

½ teaspoon vanilla extract

2 egg yolks

1 cup (8 ounces) pumpkin purée

1 cup all-purpose flour

¾ cup polenta or cornmeal

½ teaspoon ground cinnamon

¼ teaspoon ground ginger

Pinch of ground cloves

¼ teaspoon salt

¾ teaspoon baking powder

¼ teaspoon baking soda

Preheat the oven to 350°F. Spread the pumpkin seeds on a baking sheet and bake until golden brown, about 20 minutes, stirring once or twice. Remove from the pan and let cool.

In a large bowl, beat the butter and sugar together until the mixture is fluffy and pale in color. Beat in the vanilla, then the yolks one at a time, beating well after each addition. Blend in the pumpkin purée. Into a medium bowl, sift together the remaining dry ingredients. Stir the dry ingredients into the pumpkin mixture with a wooden spoon. Stir in the pumpkin seeds. Divide the dough into 3 or 4 parts. Using floured hands, roll each piece of dough into a cylinder in a sheet of parchment paper or waxed paper. Twist the ends of the paper and chill until firm, 2 or 3 hours.

Preheat the oven to 325°F. Line baking sheets with parchment paper or grease them. Unwrap the dough and slice it into ¼-inch-thick cookies. Place the cookies 1 inch apart on the prepared pans and bake for 15 to 20 minutes, or until lightly browned.

Makes about 50 cookies

Proprietor Adi Giovanetti, a native of Lucca, is a quintessential Tuscan and an uncompromising perfectionist. Along with wife Rosanna, son Francesco, and an accommodating staff, Giovanetti has worked to make constant improvements to Il Monello since its opening in 1974. The restaurant has earned three stars from the *New York Times*.

Il Monello's romantic flower-filled dining room has a collection of art that includes original paintings by Chagall, Matisse, Miró, and Dalí. The charming wine room in the back can seat private parties of twenty to thirty.

Chef Andrea Lorenzi's menu of Northern Italian cuisine is based on such superb imported Italian ingredients as scampi, radicchio, porcini, and truffles. The award-winning wine list includes more than eight hundred selections, some dating back to the 1870s.

Il Monello

THE MENU
Il Monello

*Sea Bass Rolls with Vegetables on Baby
Spinach Salad with Spicy Oil*

Sliced Steak with Beans in a Flask

Molded Chocolate Cream

Serves Eight

Sea Bass Rolls with Vegetables on Baby Spinach Salad with Spicy Oil
Rolatina di Branzino con Vegetali su Insalatina di Spinaci Novelli all' Olio Picante

Make the spicy oil for this dish at least 2 days ahead of time.

2 tablespoons extra-virgin olive oil
1 red bell pepper, cored, seeded, and diced
1 zucchini, diced
3 ounces (1 cup) white mushrooms, diced
1 garlic clove, cut into thin slices
Salt and freshly ground pepper to taste
1 cup packed fresh basil leaves
Four 8-ounce sea bass fillets, skinned
1 cup dry white wine
1 pound baby spinach leaves, stemmed
1 red onion, cut into very thin slices
Spicy Oil (recipe follows)

Preheat the oven to 350°F. In a medium sauté pan or skillet, heat the olive oil and sauté the diced pepper, zucchini, mushrooms, and garlic for 3 to 5 minutes. Season with salt and pepper. Add the basil leaves and let cool.

Cut each sea bass fillets into 6 very thin lengthwise slices. Spread a spoonful of the cooked vegetables on each slice and roll it up. Put the rolls in a baking pan, add the wine, and bake for 8 to 10 minutes, or until the fish is opaque. Make a bed of baby spinach leaves on each of 8 salad plates. Place 3 sea bass rolls on each bed of spinach. Garnish with red onion slices and sprinkle with the spicy oil.

Makes 8 servings

Il Monello

Spicy Oil
Olio Picante

1¼ cups extra-virgin olive oil
3 garlic cloves, crushed
2 tablespoons cayenne pepper
2 fresh rosemary sprigs
2 fresh basil sprigs

Add all of the ingredients to a small saucepan and warm over low heat. Remove from heat and let sit for 48 hours. Pour through a fine-meshed sieve into a jar or a bottle.

Makes 1½ cups

Sliced Steak with Beans in a Flask
Tagliata di Manzo con Fagioli al Fiasco

Sauce

2 tablespoons fresh lemon juice

2 teaspoons Worcestershire sauce

½ cup extra-virgin olive oil

Salt and freshly ground pepper to taste

1 bunch parsley, stemmed and minced

Three 1-pound T-bone steaks, about 1½ inches thick

Extra-virgin olive oil for cooking (optional)

Salt and freshly ground pepper to taste

Beans in a Flask (recipe follows)

Fresh rosemary sprigs for garnish

To make the sauce: Place the lemon juice and Worcestershire sauce in a small bowl. Whisk in the oil until the mixture is emulsified. Add the salt and pepper and stir in the parsley; set aside.

Place the steaks on a grill over a hot fire or in a large skillet filmed with olive oil over high heat. Cook for 5 minutes on each side, or until rare. Bone and cut the steaks into ½-inch-thick slices. Place the slices on an ovenproof platter or serving plates. Brush with the sauce and sprinkle with salt and pepper. Spoon the Tuscan beans alongside. Place in the preheated oven for 2 to 3 minutes to heat through. Garnish with rosemary sprigs and serve at once.

Makes 8 servings

Beans in a Flask
Fagioli al Fiasco

Traditionally these Tuscan beans are cooked in an empty Chianti bottle, but this recipe uses an earthenware pot or a heavy casserole.

2 cups (about 1 pound) dried cannellini beans
1 fresh sage sprig
1 or 2 garlic cloves, crushed
2 tablespoons extra-virgin olive oil
Salt to taste

Soak the beans in water to cover overnight. Drain and rinse the beans, and place them in a 10-cup pot with a lid or a deep, heavy casserole with a lid. Add the sage, garlic, olive oil, salt, and 4 cups water. Cover and place the pot in a baking pan. Add about 2 inches of water to the baking pan and bake in a 325°F oven for about 4 hours, adding water if needed, or until the beans are tender. Serve warm.

Makes 8 cups, or 8 to 10 servings

Molded Chocolate Cream
Bonet Piemontese

1 cup milk
1 cup heavy (whipping) cream
7 ounces *amaretti* (32 small Italian almond cookies), crumbled
Grated zest of 1 lemon
6 tablespoons unsweetened cocoa powder
Pinch of ground cinnamon
3 eggs
⅔ cup sugar

Caramel
1 cup sugar
¼ cup water

Place the milk, cream, *amaretti* crumbs, lemon zest, cocoa, and cinnamon in a medium bowl and let sit for 3 hours in the refrigerator.

To make the caramel: In a small, heavy saucepan, heat the sugar and water over medium heat, stirring, until it becomes a light golden brown. Immediately pour the caramel into a 4-cup mold, turning it to coat the bottom and sides evenly. Let cool.

Preheat the oven to 400°F. In a medium bowl, beat the eggs and sugar until the mixture is thick and pale in color. Stir the egg mixture into the milk mixture and pour into the caramel-coated mold. Place the mold in a baking pan, add hot water to the baking pan to reach halfway up the sides of the mold, and bake in the preheated oven for 1 hour. Let the dessert rest for 10 minutes before unmolding onto a serving plate. Serve cold.

Makes 8 servings

Il Monello

Since its inception nearly thirty-five years ago, La Caravelle has remained at the pinnacle of French dining in Manhattan by striking a balance between tradition and innovation. Today, chef Ono Tadashi integrates Japanese flavors and elements of classical Japanese dishes into his extraordinary French kitchen. The menu offers his brilliant and harmonious hybrids as well as dishes that La Caravelle patrons have enjoyed for decades. An extensive, mostly French wine list complements the menu. *Chef pâtissier* Laurent Richard turns out enticing and delicate French desserts, such as the Opera Cake featured in the following menu.

La Caravelle has been awarded three stars by the *New York Times*. André and Rita Jammet, now the sole owners of the restaurant, have redecorated the romantic dining room with a color scheme that gives the room an air of tranquillity and showcases the restaurant's charming murals of the parks of Paris.

THE MENU
La Caravelle

Little Flutes of Curried Escargots

Ravioli Perigord Style

Roasted Fillet of Beef with Eggplant and Plum Sauce

Opera Cake

Serves Eight

Little Flutes of Curried Escargots
Petites Flûtes d'Escargots aux Épices de Madras

1 tablespoon butter

1 tablespoon minced shallots

1 teaspoon minced garlic

1 cup (3 ounces) thinly sliced white mushrooms

1 cup (3 ounces) thinly sliced stemmed shiitake mushrooms

7 ounces canned snails, rinsed, drained, and minced

1 cup dry white wine

1 cup chicken stock (see page 202) or canned low-salt chicken broth

½ cup heavy (whipping) cream

1 teaspoon curry powder

½ cup peeled, seeded, and diced tomato

1 teaspoon minced fresh chives

1 teaspoon minced fresh parsley

12 spring roll skins, cut into quarters

In a large sauté pan or skillet, melt the butter and sauté the shallots and garlic over medium heat until translucent, about 3 minutes. Add the mushrooms and sauté for 2 more minutes. Gently stir in the minced snails. Add the wine and cook to reduce until almost dry. Add the chicken stock or broth and cook to reduce again. Add the cream, bring to a boil, and immediately remove from heat. Stir in the curry powder, tomato, chives, and parsley. Set aside and let cool.

Preheat the oven to 400°F. Lay the spring roll skins on a lightly floured work surface. Place 1 teaspoon of filling on each spring roll skin and roll up one turn, fold in the sides, and finish rolling. Transfer to a baking dish and bake in the preheated oven for 5 minutes.

Makes 48 pieces (serves 8 to 10 people)

Ravioli Perigord Style
Ravioli Perigourdine

14 ounces fresh foie gras*

Flour for dredging

2 teaspoons clarified butter (see page 202)

2 leeks, white part only, julienned

½ ounce fresh black truffle, minced

Sixteen 6-inch rounds very thin pasta dough or 16 gyoza
   (round) noodles wrappers

1 egg beaten with ½ teaspoon water

1 tablespoon butter

2 Red Delicious apples, peeled, cored, and cut into matchsticks

Pinch of ground cinnamon

2 red beets, cooked, peeled, and diced for garnish

Sauce

3 tablespoons butter

2 tablespoons minced shallots

2 teaspoons cracked or coarsely ground black pepper

1 cup port wine

1 cup veal stock (see page 207), chicken stock (see page 202),
   or canned low-salt chicken broth

½ ounce fresh or canned black truffle, minced

Vegetable oil or butter for frying

Slice the foie gras into eight ¼-inch-thick round slices with a sharp knife
that has been dipped in boiling water for each slice. Cover the slices and chill for
at least 20 minutes, or until cooking time. Dredge the foie gras slices in flour.
Film the bottom of a medium sauté pan or skillet with the clarified butter and heat
to very hot but not burning. Rapidly sauté the foie gras slices, one at a time, for
less than 1 minute on each side, or until just brown around the edges. Remove the
foie gras from the pan and set aside in a cool place. In the same pan, over
medium-high heat, sauté the leeks until soft; add the truffle and set aside.

Lay 8 pasta rounds or gyoza wrappers on a lightly floured work surface. Brush the egg and water mixture around the edges of the circles. Place 1 foie gras slice in the center of the round and arrange the leek mixture on top. Lay 1 pasta round or wrapper on top of each and press down lightly to seal.

In a small sauté pan or skillet over medium heat, melt the 1 tablespoon butter and sauté the apples until tender and golden. Stir in the cinnamon and set aside.

To make the sauce: In a medium sauté pan or skillet, melt 2 tablespoons of the butter over medium heat and sauté the shallots for 2 minutes; stir in the black pepper and port. Cook to reduce the liquid until thick enough to coat the back of a spoon; add the stock or broth, then swirl in the remaining 1 tablespoon butter. Strain the sauce through a fine-meshed sieve into a bowl and add the minced truffle. Set aside and keep warm.

Bring a large pot of salted water to a boil and poach the ravioli for 2 minutes. Remove carefully from the pan with a slotted spoon; drain and pat dry with paper towels. In a large sauté pan or skillet, heat a little oil or butter over medium-high heat and fry the ravioli quickly on both sides.

To assemble, divide the cooked apples among 8 serving plates. Top each mound with a ravioli, spoon the sauce around, and decorate with the diced beets.

Makes 8 servings

* If your specialty market cannot help you find foie gras, or goose liver, call D'Artagnan in Jersey City, New Jersey: (800) 327-8246 (phone orders are available UPS Next Day Air).

Roasted Fillet of Beef with Eggplant and Plum Sauce
Rondeau de Bœuf Barbentane

Marinade

¼ cup sake

3 tablespoons ginger sauce

3 tablespoons soy sauce

¼ cup chicken stock (see page 202) or canned low-salt chicken broth

3 tablespoons Asian sesame oil

8 garlic cloves, minced

2 Italian eggplants

Olive oil for brushing

One 2½-pound beef tenderloin

2 teaspoons butter

Plum Sauce

½ cup mirin (Japanese sweet rice wine)

3 tablespoons Chinese plum sauce

½ cup veal stock (see page 207), or chicken stock (see page 202),
   or canned low-salt chicken broth

3 tablespoons beet purée

3 tablespoons butter

To make the marinade: In a large saucepan, combine all the ingredients for the marinade and set aside.

Slice the eggplant into twenty-four ⅓-inch-thick rounds. Brush the eggplant slices with olive oil and grill or pan-fry them over high heat to brown them. Add the eggplant slices to the marinade and cook over medium-high heat until soft, about 2 minutes. With a metal spatula, remove the eggplant from the marinade, cover, and keep warm.

Cut the tenderloin into 16 slices. In a skillet or sauté pan, melt the butter over medium-high heat and cook the beef slices for 2 minutes on each side, turning once. Remove from heat and cover with aluminum foil to keep warm.

To make the plum sauce: In a small saucepan, boil the mirin over high heat for 2 or 3 minutes. Stir in the plum sauce, stock or broth, and beet purée, and boil for 1 minute. Whisk in the butter.

On each of 8 serving plates, alternate layers of eggplant and beef, starting and finishing with the eggplant. Spoon the warm sauce around. Serve at once.

Makes 8 servings

Opera Cake
Gâteau d'Opera Saint-Brisson
(Created by pastry chef Laurent Richard)

This exquisite dessert was originally created at the famous Café de la Paix in Paris for the premiere gala of an opera.

Cake

1 cup sugar

5 egg yolks

7 large egg whites

1¼ cups unbleached all-purpose flour

6 tablespoons clarified butter (see page 202), melted

Sugar Syrup

1 cup water

1 cup sugar

Coffee extract or cold brewed espresso to taste

Double Ganache

1 cup heavy (whipping) cream

7 ounces semisweet chocolate, chopped

Mocha Butter Cream

3 medium eggs

⅞ cup sugar

¼ cup water

2¾ sticks butter at room temperature

Coffee extract or cold brewed espresso to taste

Mocha Sauce (recipe follows)

To make the cake: Preheat the oven to 450°F. Butter one 11-by-17-inch sheet pan and dust thoroughly with flour; knock out the excess flour.

In a large bowl, gradually beat the sugar into the egg yolks and continue

88

beating for several minutes until the mixture is thick and pale in color.

In another large bowl, beat the egg whites until soft peaks form. Gently fold the egg whites into the yolk mixture, gradually adding the flour as you fold. When almost blended, fold in the clarified butter by spoonfuls. Do not overmix or the egg whites will deflate.

Pour the butter into the prepared pan, tilting to fill to the rim. Set the pan in the middle of the preheated oven and bake for 10 to 14 minutes, or until the cake is springy to the touch and just beginning to shrink from the edges of the pan. Remove the cake from the oven and let cool in the pan for 10 minutes; unmold onto a wire rack.

To make the sugar syrup: In a large, heavy saucepan over high heat, bring the water and sugar to a boil, swirling the pan to dissolve the sugar completely. Remove from heat, let cool, and add the coffee extract or espresso. Cover and refrigerate.

To make the ganache: In a large, heavy saucepan, bring the cream to a boil. Add the chocolate and whisk until melted and smooth. Remove from heat, pour through a fine-meshed sieve, and let cool to room temperature. Cover and refrigerate.

To make the butter cream: In a large bowl, beat the eggs until they are thick and pale in color; set aside. In a heavy saucepan, bring the sugar and water to a simmer over medium-high heat, swirling the pan to dissolve the sugar completely. Cover tightly and boil to the soft-ball stage (a drop of the mixture falling from a spoon into a cup of cold water will form a soft ball).

Whisk the hot syrup into the beaten eggs in a thin stream. Set the bowl in a pan of almost-simmering water and beat for 4 to 5 minutes, or until a slowly dissolving ribbon is formed on the surface of the mixture when the beaters are lifted.

In a large bowl, beat the butter until it is fluffy. Beat the butter into the egg mixture in small increments until smooth. Stir in the coffee extract or espresso. Place the bowl in a large bowl of ice water and beat until the cream firms to an easy spreading consistency. Use at once, or cover and store in the refrigerator for up to 3 days, or freeze for several weeks. Let come to room temperature before using.

To assemble the cake: Dust the surface of a large baking pan with sugar. Place a pastry ring or springform cake ring over the sheet of cake and cut around the inside of the ring. Repeat to form a second circle from the sheet of cake. Place the ring in the sugar-dusted pan and insert 1 cake layer in it. Spoon some of the sugar syrup over the cake and let the syrup be absorbed. Spread the cake with a layer of butter cream. Place the second cake layer over the butter cream. Spoon some more sugar syrup over the top layer of cake. Coat with a thin layer of ganache. Cover and refrigerate until serving time.

Remove the cake from the refrigerator 10 minutes before serving. Soak a towel in warm water, wring out the moisture, and apply it to the ring, then remove the ring from the cake. Cut the cake with a knife dipped in hot water. Serve with the mocha sauce. The cake will keep, covered, in the refrigerator for a day or two.

Makes 1 cake

Mocha Sauce

8 egg yolks
½ cup plus 1 tablespoon sugar
3 cups milk
1 vanilla bean, split lengthwise, or 1 teaspoon vanilla extract
Coffee extract or cold brewed espresso to taste

In a large bowl, beat together the egg yolks and sugar until the mixture is thick and pale in color. In a small saucepan, heat the milk and scrape in the seeds from the vanilla bean, if using. Cut the bean into pieces, add the pieces to the milk, and bring to a gentle boil. Remove from heat and strain the cream through a fine-meshed sieve. Pour a little of the milk into the yolk mixture and whisk together. Whisk the yolk mixture into the milk and cook over low heat until the mixture thickens enough to coat the back of spoon; do not let the mixture boil. Remove from heat and add the vanilla extract, if using, and the coffee extract or espresso. Let cool, cover, and refrigerate until serving time.

La Caravelle

La Côte Basque

La Côte Basque has consistently ranked at the top of the list of the best French restaurants in Manhattan. Chef-proprietor Jean-Jacques Rachou, known for his exacting standards, attracts Culinary Institute of America graduates who want the best classical cooking foundation they can find. Chef Rachou uses superb ingredients to create dishes that artistically blend flavor, color, and texture. His imaginative and personal adaptation of classic French cuisine has earned the restaurant three stars from the *New York Times*. Rachou bought La Côte Basque from its previous owners in 1980, at which time he remodeled the restaurant but preserved Bernard Lamotte's lovely murals of coastal France.

THE MENU

La Côte Basque

Cream of Basil Soup

Scottish Salmon with Asparagus

Rack of Lamb with Thyme

Puff Pastry with Mixed Fruit

Serves Four

Cream of Basil Soup
Crème au Basilic Germiny

3 cups chicken consommé, stock (see page 202), or canned
   low-salt chicken broth
1 bunch fresh basil, stemmed and minced
2 egg yolks
1⅓ cups crème fraîche (see page 203)

In a large saucepan, bring the consommé, stock, or broth to a boil. Add the basil and cook for 3 minutes; set aside.

In a large bowl, beat the egg yolks and crème fraîche together. In a slow, steady stream, pour the hot consommé, stock, or broth into the egg mixture, whisking constantly. Return the mixture to the saucepan and cook over low heat, stirring constantly, until it thickens enough to lightly coat the back of a spoon. (Do not allow the mixture to boil or even to simmer while cooking, or it will curdle.) Remove from heat, ladle the soup into 4 bowls, and serve at once.

Makes 4 servings

Scottish Salmon with Asparagus
Saumon d'Écosse aux Asperges

Serve these asparagus-laced slices of salmon with steamed potatoes or fresh pasta.

2 pounds asparagus
One 1½-pound salmon fillet, skinned
6 tablespoons butter
1 leek, white part only, minced
2 tablespoons minced shallots
14 ounces mushrooms
½ cup dry white wine
½ cup cooking liquid from the asparagus
½ cup crème fraîche (see page 203)
Salt and freshly ground pepper to taste

Peel the asparagus and cut off the top 2 inches of each spear. (Reserve the stems for another use.) Bring a large pot of water to a boil and cook the asparagus until crisp-tender, 8 to 10 minutes. Drain and pat dry. Using a small, pointed knife, insert the asparagus tips lengthwise into the salmon fillet. Cut the fillet into 8 slices.

In a large sauté pan or skillet, melt the butter and sauté the leek, shallot, and mushrooms over medium heat for 5 minutes. Add the wine and cooking liquid from the asparagus and raise the heat to high. Cook to reduce the liquid until dry and set aside. Steam the salmon slices over boiling water in a covered pan until just opaque, 3 or 4 minutes; set aside.

Add the crème fraîche to the leek mixture and season with salt and pepper. Transfer the mixture to a blender or food processor and purée to a sauce. Spoon a pool of the sauce in the center of each serving plate and top with 2 slices of salmon. Serve warm.

Makes 4 servings

Rack of Lamb with Thyme
Carre d'Agneau au Thym

Ask your butcher to "French-cut" the racks of lamb. Save all the bones and meat trimmings.

2 racks of lamb
Salt, freshly ground pepper, and minced fresh thyme to taste
2 tablespoons vegetable oil
Natural Lamb Stock (recipe follows)

Sprinkle the racks of lamb with the salt, pepper, and thyme, and rub the seasoning gently into the meat. Wrap the exposed bones tightly with aluminum foil.

Preheat the oven and roasting pan to 450°F. Add the vegetable oil and the lamb, meat-side down, to the roasting pan. Place in the oven and reduce the temperature to 400°F. After 2 or 3 minutes, turn the racks onto their fat side. Continue to roast the lamb for a total of 25 to 27 minutes for medium rare.

Remove the lamb from the oven and let it rest at room temperature for 5 to 8 minutes. Remove the aluminum foil and carve the lamb. Serve with the lamb stock on the side.

Makes 4 servings

Natural Lamb Stock
Jus d'Agneau

Bones and trimmings from racks of lamb
1 onion, diced
2 carrots, peeled and diced
2 celery stalks, diced
4 or 5 garlic cloves, minced
½ to 1 teaspoon minced fresh thyme, plus more to taste
2 bay leaves
½ to 1 teaspoon minced fresh rosemary leaves
6 plum tomatoes, chopped
6 whole peppercorns
Salt to taste

Preheat the oven to 400°F. Place the bones and trimmings in a baking pan and roast in the preheated oven for 30 to 40 minutes, or until well browned. Remove from the oven and pour the fat out of the pan.

To a stockpot or large saucepan, add the bones, diced vegetables, garlic, thyme bay leaves, rosemary, tomatoes, peppercorns, and water to cover. Bring to a gentle boil, skimming off any foam that rises to the top. Lower heat, cover, and simmer for 3 to 4 hours.

Strain the stock through a sieve into a large saucepan over high heat. Season with salt and reduce the liquid slightly if the flavor is weak. Stir in a little more fresh thyme.

Makes about 3 cups

La Côte Basque

Puff Pastry with Mixed Fruit
Feuilletée aux Fruits

12 ounces homemade puff pastry (see page 37) or thawed frozen puff pastry
2 egg yolks, beaten
Sifted confectioners' sugar for sprinkling
2 apples
3 tablespoons butter
½ cup Grand Marnier
2 kiwi fruits, peeled and sliced
2 oranges, peeled and sectioned (see page 206)
1 cup fresh strawberries, hulled
½ cup fresh raspberries
Caramel Sauce (recipe follows)

Preheat the oven to 400°F for at least 20 minutes. Cover a baking sheet with parchment paper or grease the sheet with butter.

On a lightly floured pastry board, roll out the puff pastry dough ⅛ inch thick. Cover the dough and chill for 20 minutes. Cut out four 2- to 3-inch-diameter circles and cut the circles in half. Place the half-circles on the prepared baking sheet and brush them lightly with the beaten egg yolks.

Bake in the preheated oven for 25 minutes, or until golden. Remove the pastry from the oven and sprinkle with confectioners' sugar. Raise the oven temperature to 425°F and return the pastry to the oven until the sugar is glazed. Remove from the oven and lower the oven temperature to 325°F.

Cut each apple into 6 wedges. Using a paring knife, peel and trim the wedges into large olive shapes. In a large skillet or sauté pan, melt the butter over medium heat and sauté the apples until tender, about 5 minutes. Add the Grand Marnier, let it warm, and ignite it with a match; shake the pan until the flames have subsided; set aside.

Using a serrated knife, cut the pastries in half and place the raspberries inside. Warm in the 325°F oven for about 10 minutes. Pool some of the caramel sauce onto each plate. Place 1 pastry in the center of the sauce and arrange one fourth of the apples, kiwis, oranges, and strawberries around it. Sprinkle the fruit with a little of the Grand Marnier left in the pan. Lightly powder the top of each pastry with confectioners' sugar and serve.

Makes 4 servings

Caramel Sauce

½ cup sugar
1 tablespoon butter
2 cups half-and-half
5 egg yolks
¼ cup Grand Marnier

In a heavy, medium saucepan, stir the sugar and butter together constantly over medium heat until the mixture is golden brown, watching carefully to keep it from burning. In a steady stream, whisk in the half-and-half, bring it to a boil, and remove from heat.

In another medium saucepan, whisk together the 5 egg yolks. Gradually whisk in the caramel mixture. Place the saucepan over medium-high heat and simmer for 1 minute. Remove from heat and stir in the Grand Marnier. Serve warm. To store, let cool and refrigerate for up to 1 week.

Makes about 2 cups

LE BERNARDIN

For lovers of fish dishes, one Manhattan restaurant has achieved preeminence. Le Bernardin has received rare accolades since its opening in 1986, including four stars from the *New York Times* and five diamonds from the American Automobile Association. It is one of only seven United States restaurants listed in *Traditions et Qualité*.

Le Bernardin was an acclaimed restaurant in Paris before sister and brother Maguy and Gilbert Le Coze moved it to its present midtown address in 1986 as the culinary centerpiece for the newly opened Equitable Center. Today diners enjoy the exquisitely flavored and beautifully presented creations of chef Eric Ripert, whose training began with schooling in France and has included stints at Tour d'Argent, Jamin, Jean Louis, and Bouley. A native of Andorra, Ripert has brought flavors from the South of France and Spain to Le Bernardin. Imaginative pastry chef Herve Poussot creates ravishing desserts such as the one featured in the following menu.

THE MENU
Le Bernardin

Seared Tuna and Truffled Herb Salad

Fricassee of Shellfish

Fillet of Black Bass in a Scallion and Ginger Nage

Chinese spiced Red Snapper with Port Sauce and Cèpes

Chocolate Dome with a Symphony of Crème Brûlée on a Macaroon

Serves Four

Seared Tuna and Truffled Herb Salad

Vinaigrette
3 tablespoons balsamic vinegar
1 canned black truffle, drained (juice reserved) and minced
1 tablespoon truffle juice
7 tablespoons extra-virgin olive oil
Salt and freshly ground pepper to taste

One 12-ounce tuna loin
1 tablespoon minced fresh thyme
Salt and freshly ground pepper to taste
Oil for searing
4 cups assorted baby greens
1 cup mixed fresh herbs such as basil, dill, and parsley

To make the vinaigrette: In a small bowl, whisk together the balsamic vinegar, minced truffle, truffle juice, and olive oil. Season with salt and pepper and set aside.

Season the tuna with the thyme, salt, and pepper. Film a large sauté pan or skillet with oil and sear the tuna over high heat until it is crusty on the outside and rare in the center.

Slice the seared tuna into ¼-inch-thick slices and arrange the slices on the 4 plates. Garnish with the baby greens and fresh herbs. Drizzle the vinaigrette over everything and serve.

Makes 4 servings

Fricassee of Shellfish

1¼ pounds mussels (small cultured Rope mussels preferred)

32 littleneck clams

32 Manila clams

12 bay scallops in the shell

12 oysters such as Belon or Cotuit

1 cup (2 sticks) unsalted butter at room temperature

2 garlic cloves, minced

2 shallots, minced

3 tablespoons minced fresh parsley

½ cup dry white wine

Freshly ground black pepper to taste

12 tomatoes, cored and chopped

1 to 2 cups water

1½ cups heavy (whipping) cream

Salt to taste

Juice of 1 lemon

Minced fresh parsley to taste

Wash the shellfish in salted water and clean the beards from the mussels. Set aside in the refrigerator.

In a medium bowl, cream the butter until it is fluffy. Beat in the garlic, shallots, parsley, white wine, and pepper. Mix until completely smooth and set aside.

In a blender or food processor, purée the tomatoes. Force the purée through the fine screen of a food mill or a fine-meshed sieve. You should have about 3 cups of tomato purée; set aside.

Just before serving, add the water to a large pot and bring to a boil. Add all the shellfish except the oysters. Cover and steam just until the shellfish open.

At the same time, in a large saucepan, bring the tomato purée to a boil, then stir in the heavy cream. Reduce the heat to low and simmer for 4 minutes. Add

Le Bernardin

the garlic-herb butter to the tomato mixture; raise the heat to high and boil until the mixture has emulsified; set aside and keep warm.

Preheat the oven to 400°F. To shuck the oysters, place 1 oyster, curved-side down, on a work surface with the hinge end of the oyster facing you. Insert an oyster knife or beer can opener into the gap at the hinge. Press down on the handle while holding the oyster with your other hand, and the hinge will pop open. Insert a small knife inside the top shell where the muscle is attached and scrape through the muscle to release the oyster. Lift up the front of the top shell and bend it toward the hinge to snap it free. Place the oysters in a baking dish and bake in the preheated oven for 1 minute.

Divide the shellfish and oysters equally among 4 large, deep plates. Strain the cooking juices from the shellfish into the butter sauce; season with salt and a good amount of pepper. Add the lemon juice and minced parsley. Spoon the sauce over the hot shellfish and serve.

Makes 4 servings

Fillet of Black Bass in a Scallion and Ginger Nage

8 cups Nage (recipe follows)
Four 6-ounce black bass or sea bass fillets
20 green onions, chopped
3½ ounces julienned fresh ginger
1 lemon, diced
1 tomato, peeled and cut into 1½-inch dice
10 fresh cilantro leaves, julienned

In a large saucepan over medium heat, bring 4 cups of the *nage* to a simmer over medium heat. Add the fillets and poach for 3 minutes. Carefully remove the fish fillets with a slotted spoon and place them in a deep dish.

In the same pan that was used to poach the fish, blanch the green onions for 20 seconds. Top the fish with the green onions, ginger, lemon, tomato, and cilantro. Finally, bring the remaining nage to a boil and pour it over the fish.

Makes 4 servings

Nage

4 cups dry white wine
1 cup white wine vinegar
1 celery stalk
1 garlic clove
4 leeks
3 tomatoes
1 fresh thyme sprig
1 fresh rosemary sprig
Sea salt and cayenne pepper to taste
2 fennel branches
3 fresh mint sprigs
1 fresh basil sprig

Into a large saucepan or stockpot, place the wine, vinegar, celery, garlic, leeks, tomatoes, herbs, salt, and cayenne and bring to a boil. Reduce heat to low and simmer for 1½ hours without covering. Towards the end, add the fennel, mint, and basil. Remove from the heat and let sit until all of the flavors have blended, about 30 minutes.

Le Bernardin

Chinese-spiced Red Snapper with Port Sauce and Cèpes

Cèpe is the French name for the bolete, or porcino mushroom. Fresh porcini mushrooms are found in specialty foods stores, usually during the fall, winter, and spring.

Port Sauce
2½ cups port
2½ cups sherry wine vinegar
½ cup (1 stick) unsalted butter, cut into 8 pieces
Salt and freshly ground pepper to taste

¼ cup five-spice powder (preferably Hong Lu brand)
Four 7-ounce red snapper fillets
5 tablespoons peanut oil
Salt and freshly ground pepper to taste
4 cèpe mushrooms, thinly sliced
1 teaspoon butter
1 shallot, minced
½ tablespoon minced fresh parsley
½ tablespoon minced fresh thyme

To make the sauce: In a medium saucepan, cook the port over medium heat to reduce it to a syrupy consistency; be careful not to caramelize it. Add the vinegar and cook the mixture again to reduce it to a syrupy consistency. Whisk in the butter 1 tablespoon at a time; the sauce will thicken and emulsify. Add salt and pepper and keep warm over barely tepid water.

Sprinkle the five-spice powder on all sides of the fish fillets. In a large sauté pan or skillet, heat 4 tablespoons of the peanut oil over high heat and sauté the fillets on each side until they are crisp, firm to touch, and opaque throughout. Remove from heat, sprinkle with salt and pepper, and set aside. Cover and keep warm.

In a medium sauté pan or skillet, heat the remaining 1 tablespoon peanut oil over medium heat and sauté the cèpes for 5 minutes. Stir in the butter and

Le Bernardin

shallot and cook another 2 minutes. Stir in the parsley, thyme, salt, and pepper.

To serve, arrange the cèpes in the center of each of 4 plates. Place a fillet on top of each serving of cèpes, spoon the sauce over, and serve.

Makes 4 servings

Chocolate Dome with a Symphony of Crème Brûlée on a Macaroon

Crème Brûlée

⅔ cup heavy (whipping) cream

½ cup milk

½ vanilla bean split lengthwise, or 1 teaspoon vanilla extract

4 egg yolks

⅓ cup sugar

Chocolate Mousse

9 ounces semisweet chocolate, chopped

3 tablespoons sugar

2 teaspoons vanilla extract

3 cups whipped cream

Macaroons

1 cup (4 ounces) ground almonds

2 cups confectioners' sugar

3 egg whites

To make the crème brûlée: Preheat the oven to 325°F. In a small, heavy saucepan, bring the cream and milk to a boil; remove from heat. If you are using a vanilla bean half, scrape in the vanilla bean pulp and cut the bean in half crosswise. Add the bean pieces to the milk and cream mixture, cover, and let sit for 10 minutes.

In a medium bowl, whisk together the egg yolks and sugar until slightly thickened. Stir in the hot cream mixture, and the vanilla extract, if using. Strain the custard into a 2-cup ramekin. Set the ramekin in a baking dish and pour water into the dish to halfway up the sides of the ramekin. Bake in the preheated oven for 20 minutes, or until the custard is set but quivers slightly when shaken. Refrigerate for several hours, or until thoroughly chilled.

To make the chocolate mousse: In a double boiler over barely simmering water, melt the chocolate. Beat in the sugar and vanilla. Remove from heat and let cool slightly. Gently fold in the whipped cream. Cover and chill in the refrigerator for several hours.

To make the macaroons: Preheat the oven to 350°F. Line a baking sheet with aluminum foil and set aside. In a medium bowl, mix together the almonds and sugar and sift them through a fine-meshed sieve. In a deep bowl, beat the egg whites until foamy. Gradually add the sugar and almonds while beating until soft peaks form. Place this mixture in a pastry bag fitted with a ¾-inch tube tip. Pipe 3-inch-diameter macaroons about 1 inch apart onto the prepared baking sheet. Bake the macaroons in the preheated oven for 8 minutes, or until they are barely light brown. Remove from the oven and let cool completely on the foil. When completely cool, use a metal spatula to remove the macaroons from the foil.

To assemble, fill one of 6 bombe molds or other dome-shaped molds halfway full with the chocolate mousse. Next add the crème brûlée and finish with a macaroon. Repeat this process for the remaining 5 molds. Refrigerate the molds for several hours. Remove the molds by dipping them briefly into hot water. Cover and refrigerate the bombes until serving time.

Makes 6 servings

Le Cirque, one of the most cherished restaurants in the world, turns out extraordinary performances for demanding audiences day after day. Under the assured guidance of famed restaurateur Sirio Maccioni, Le Cirque has consistently rated four stars from the *New York Times*. Extraordinary dishes, ranging from classical French to variations on contemporary haute cuisine, are served in an exciting, elegant, and cheerful atmosphere. The energy in the dining room is unique and completely New York: a combination of celebrity and power that is as remarkable as the food from the backstage kitchen. Le Cirque's exhaustive list of French, American, and Italian wines is one of the best in the world.

Executive chef Sylvain Portay's cooking is based on classic French technique with an Italian influence and an emphasis on vegetables. Pastry chef Jacques Torres was awarded the prestigious title of Chef Pâtissier Meilleur Ouvrier de France. He is given free reign in the pastry kitchen with one directive: to not change Le Cirque's legendary crème brûlée. Based on a two-hundred-year-old recipe Sirio Maccioni brought back from Barcelona, this signature dish has been perfected at the restaurant over the years, and many ramekins of the glazed custard are sold every day. (This recipe is included in the following menu.) Sirio Maccioni is determined that Le Cirque will continue to set trends and to raise standards while preserving the best of its past.

Le Cirque

THE MENU
Le Cirque

Sea Scallop Fantasy in Black Tie

Crisp Sea Bass Wrapped in Potatoes with a Barolo Wine Sauce

Lamb Stew with Orange Zest and Rosemary

Crème Brûlée

Serves Four

Sea Scallop Fantasy in Black Tie
Fantaisie de St-Jacques en Habit Noir

16 sea scallops (1 ounce each)
2 or 3 fresh or canned truffles (1 ounce each)
¼ cup white vermouth, preferably Noilly-Prat
1 tablespoon heavy (whipping) cream
10 tablespoons unsalted butter
Salt and freshly ground pepper to taste
1 bunch spinach (8 ounces), stemmed
2 tablespoons minced fresh chervil

Trim the muscle on the sides of the sea scallops if necessary; reserve the muscle. Rinse the sea scallops and pat them dry with paper towels. Cut each scallop crosswise into four ¼-inch-thick slices.

Preheat the oven to 300°F. If using canned truffles, drain them and reserve the juice. With a truffle slicer or potato peeler, cut the truffles into about 50 paper-thin slices no larger in diameter than the scallops. Place 1 truffle slice between each slice of scallop and reassemble the scallop; for each one there will be 4 slices of scallop and 3 slices of truffle. Chop the scraps of leftover truffles.

In a small saucepan, cook the vermouth and any reserved muscles over medium heat until dry. Reduce heat to low, add any reserved truffle juice and the cream, and whisk in 8 tablespoons of the butter 1 tablespoon at a time; the sauce will thicken and emulsify. Add the salt and pepper and place the pan over barely tepid water to keep the sauce warm.

Melt the remaining 2 tablespoons butter. Place the spinach leaves in a bowl and toss them with 1 tablespoon of the melted butter. Arrange the spinach leaves on a serving plate and place them in the preheated oven for 2 or 3 minutes, or until they are slightly wilted; set aside.

Sprinkle the scallops with salt and pepper. In a large nonstick pan, heat the remaining 1 tablespoon of melted butter over medium heat and sauté the

Le Cirque

scallops on one side for 3 minutes. Turn the scallops over, lower the heat, and sauté them for another 3 minutes.

If you like, cut each scallop in half horizontally so you can see the layers of black and white. Arrange the scallops on top of the spinach leaves. Add the minced truffles to the butter sauce and coat each scallop with the sauce. Sprinkle with the chervil and serve.

Makes 4 servings

Crisp Sea Bass Wrapped in Potatoes with a Barolo Wine Sauce
Paupiette de Sea Bass Croustillante, Sauce au Vin de Barolo

1 bottle Barolo wine
3 shallots, minced
1 fresh thyme sprig
1 tablespoon heavy (whipping) cream
½ cup (1 stick) butter, cut into 8 tablespoon-sized pieces
2 leeks, cut into thin slices
Salt and freshly ground pepper to taste
2 very large potatoes, peeled
¼ cup clarified butter (see page 202)
Two 2-pound sea bass fillets, skinned
Pinch of sugar
1 tablespoon minced fresh chives

In a small saucepan, cook the red wine, shallots, and thyme over high heat until the wine is almost evaporated. Stir in the cream and set aside.

In a small sauté pan or skillet, melt 2 tablespoons of the solid butter and sauté the leeks over medium heat until soft, about 5 minutes. Add salt and pepper; set aside.

Cut the potatoes into very thin lengthwise slices with a mandoline. Toss the potato slices with 2 tablespoons of the clarified butter and a touch of salt. Sprinkle the fillets with salt and pepper and form them into 1 compact and rectangular shape. On a piece of parchment paper or aluminum foil, overlap the potato slices to form a rectangle. Place the rectangle of fish on top of the potato slices and wrap it in the slices; cover with the paper or foil and refrigerate.

If the fish is more than ½ inch thick, preheat the oven to 400°F. Over low heat, bring the reduced wine mixture to a boil. Whisk in the remaining 6 tablespoons solid butter 1 tablespoon at a time, then the salt, pepper, and a pinch of sugar. Strain the sauce through a fine-meshed sieve; set aside and keep warm over barely tepid water.

Le Cirque

In a large nonstick pan, heat the remaining 2 tablespoons of clarified butter over medium heat and sauté paupiette for 2 to 3 minutes on each side, or until golden brown. If the fish is more than ½ inch thick, place it in the preheated oven to bake until just opaque.

To serve, place the leeks in the center of the plate, spoon the sauce around, and arrange the paupiette on top. Sprinkle with chives and serve at once.

Makes 4 servings

Lamb Stew with Orange Zest and Rosemary
Navarin d'Agneau aux Zestes d'Orange et Romarin

Serve this aromatic stew with a side dish of pasta tossed with butter and minced fresh basil.

1 orange
1 lamb shoulder, trimmed and cut into 1-inch cubes
Salt and freshly ground pepper to taste
3 tablespoons oil
1 fresh rosemary sprig
2 garlic cloves
2 tablespoons all-purpose flour
1 tablespoon tomato paste
½ cup dry white wine
1 tablespoon Curaçao or Grand Marnier
Chicken stock (see page 202) or canned low-salt chicken broth to cover
2 bunches baby carrots, peeled
1 pound turnips, each trimmed into an elongated oval
6 ounces pearl onions, peeled
1 celery stalk, peeled and cut into ½-inch-thick slices
6 ounces haricots verts or baby Blue Lake green beans
6 ounces fresh or frozen peas
1 tablespoon butter

Preheat the oven to 400°F. Grate the zest of one half of the orange and cut the remaining zest into julienne. Set the grated zest aside and blanch the julienned zest in boiling water for 10 minutes; drain and set aside.

Sprinkle the lamb with salt and pepper. In a heavy, ovenproof casserole, heat the oil and brown the lamb cubes on all sides over medium-high heat. Add the rosemary sprig, grated orange zest, and garlic, and cook until the garlic is translucent, about 3 minutes. Sprinkle the flour over and stir to blend.

Place the casserole in the preheated oven for 10 minutes, then remove it from the oven and reduce the oven temperature to 350°F. Place the casserole

Le Cirque

over medium heat and stir in the tomato paste. Stir in the white wine and Curaçao or Grand Marnier, and cook to reduce by one third. Pour in enough chicken stock or broth to cover the lamb by 1 inch. Stir again to make sure that the sauce is not sticking to the bottom of the casserole, then add the carrots, turnips, onions, and celery.

Cover the casserole, place in the 350°F oven, and bake for 2 hours, or until the lamb is tender. Meanwhile, blanch the haricots verts or Blue Lake beans in boiling salted water for 3 minutes. Drain, rinse under cold water, drain again, and set aside.

Just before serving, remove the meat and vegetables from the casserole. Strain the sauce and return it to the casserole Add the peas, beans, and the julienned orange zest, and reheat for a few minutes. If the sauce seems too thick, add a little water. Finish the sauce by stirring in the butter. Return the meat and other vegetables to the pan, heat for a few minutes, and serve.

Makes 4 servings

Crème Brûlée

3 cups heavy (whipping) cream
1 vanilla bean, split lengthwise
½ cup granulated sugar
6 egg yolks
6 tablespoons packed brown sugar

Preheat the oven to 250°F. In a heavy saucepan, heat the cream over medium heat. Scrape the pulp from the vanilla bean into the cream, then cut the bean into 2-inch pieces and add the pieces to the pan. Bring the cream to a simmer, remove from heat, and set aside.

In a large bowl, whisk together the granulated sugar and egg yolks until the mixture is thick and pale in color. Pour the cream into the egg mixture in a slow, steady stream, whisking constantly. Strain through a fine-meshed sieve and pour the custard into a 5-cup heatproof mold. Place the mold in a baking dish and pour warm water into the dish to halfway up the sides of the mold. Cover with aluminum foil and bake in the preheated oven for 1 hour, or just until set. Refrigerate for several hours, or until thoroughly chilled.

Just before serving, preheat the broiler. Place the brown sugar in a fine-meshed sieve and push the sugar through with the back of a spoon to evenly layer the top of the custard. Place the custard under the broiler about 2 inches from the heat until the sugar is melted and crisp, about 30 seconds to 1 minute, being careful not to burn it. Let cool for a few minutes, then serve.

Makes 4 to 6 servings

Lutèce

The legendary reputation and popularity of Lutèce is the result of the dedication of its renowned yet down-to-earth master chef, André Soltner. His celebrated restaurant has received four stars from the *New York Times* and five stars from the Mobil Travel Guide. Chef Soltner has been awarded the Meilleur Ouvrier de France for excellence in his craft.

Lutèce—whose name comes from Lutetia, the ancient name for Paris— opened in 1961. André Soltner has been cooking at Lutèce since its opening and became its sole owner in 1972. Simone Soltner is at her husband's side managing the busy reservations desk and ensuring memorable service. Chef Soltner brings great enthusiasm and fortitude to his work and is sincerely concerned about the happiness of his guests while they are under his roof. "I cook for love," he says. "Between me and the customer is an invisible string, a special rapport."

Soltner adheres to classic French cooking traditions, plus an occasional specialty from his native Alsace. Consider the chef's *dégustation,* or tasting menu, or ask chef Soltner to cook you whatever he pleases; it will be an experience to remember for a long time.

Lutèce's comfortable East Side brownstone setting includes a charming bar room up front, an airy main garden dining room in the back, and two small, more formal rooms upstairs. The following menu will bring a taste of Lutèce to your home.

Lutèce

THE MENU
Lutèce

Almond Soup

Cold Marinated Salmon on Cucumber Salad

Caramelized Rack of Lamb

Pears with Calvados

Serves Four

Almond Soup
Soupe aux Amandes

1 cup (5½ ounces) blanched almonds, plus ¼ cup toasted almonds
   (see page 206) for garnish
3 hard-cooked egg yolks
3 cups heavy (whipping) cream
4 cups chicken stock (see page 202) or canned low-salt chicken
   broth, heated
2 raw egg yolks
Salt and freshly ground pepper to taste

In a blender or food processor, process the almonds and hard-cooked egg yolks to a smooth paste. In a large saucepan, stir together the almond mixture and 1½ cups of the cream. Add the chicken stock or broth and bring to a boil. Reduce heat to low and simmer the mixture for 5 minutes.

Meanwhile, in another large saucepan, whisk together the remaining 1½ cups cream and the 2 raw egg yolks. After the stock or broth mixture has simmered, pour the cream mixture into it and whisk the soup over medium heat for 2 minutes; do not let it boil. Season with salt and pepper, sprinkle with toasted almonds, and serve at once.

Makes 4 servings

Cold Marinated Salmon on Cucumber Salad
Saumon Mariné sur Salade de Concombre

This recipe should be started 12 hours before serving time.

One 1¼-pound salmon fillet, skinned
2¼ teaspoons salt
¾ teaspoon sugar
2 tablespoons minced fresh dill
¾ teaspoon coarsely ground white pepper
¼ cup olive oil, plus 2½ teaspoons
1 medium cucumber, peeled
½ teaspoon white wine vinegar
½ tablespoon crème fraîche (see page 203)
Salt and freshly ground black pepper to taste
Fresh dill sprigs for garnish

Twelve hours before serving: Remove any bones from the salmon and place the salmon in a large, shallow nonaluminum dish. In a small bowl, stir together the salt, sugar, minced dill, pepper, and ¼ cup olive oil. Coat the salmon with this mixture and refrigerate, covered, for 12 hours. From time to time spoon the liquid that is produced over the salmon.

Cut the cucumber in half lengthwise. With a spoon, scrape out the seeds and discard them. Thinly slice the cucumber and set aside. In a small bowl, whisk together the remaining 2½ teaspoons olive oil, vinegar, the crème fraîche, salt, and pepper. Add the cucumber slices and stir together.

Cut the marinated salmon into very thin slices. Divide the cucumber salad among 4 plates and top with the salmon slices. Garnish with dill sprigs and serve.

Makes 4 servings

Caramelized Rack of Lamb
Carre d'Agneau Caramelisé

Serve this honey-glazed rack of lamb with green beans and potatoes.

2 racks of lamb (8 chops each)
2 tablespoons honey
2 scant tablespoons Dijon mustard
2 teaspoons dried thyme, crumbled
Juice of 1 lemon
2 tablespoons peanut oil
Salt and freshly ground black pepper to taste
2 small onions, cut into ⅓-inch-thick wedges
2 carrots, peeled and cut into ⅓-inch pieces
2 unpeeled garlic cloves
1½ cups dry white wine or water
Watercress sprigs for garnish

Have your butcher prepare the rack of lamb by removing most of the fat and the chine (backbone). Have the rib bones French cut (so that they extend from the meat by ¾ inch). Ask the butcher to give you the chine and rib ends along with the racks.

Preheat the oven to 375°F. In a small bowl, stir together the honey, Dijon mustard, thyme, and lemon juice; set aside. Brush the lamb with the peanut oil and sprinkle with salt and pepper. Place the racks in a roasting pan and surround with the reserved bones. Roast in the preheated oven for 4 minutes, then turn and baste the meat. Roast another 4 minutes, then turn, baste the meat, and roast another 4 minutes. Add the onions, carrots, and garlic to the roasting pan and roast for 5 minutes. Turn and baste the meat, stir the vegetables and bones, and roast another 5 minutes. Place the lamb on a platter and let sit in a warm place for 5 to 6 minutes; leave the bones and vegetables in the roasting pan.

Meanwhile, preheat the broiler. Pour all the fat from the roasting pan. Add the wine or water to the bones and vegetables. Place the pan over high heat and boil the liquid for a few minutes, stirring the bones and vegetables with a wooden spoon. When the liquid has been reduced by half, strain it through a sieve into a sauceboat. Press the vegetables through the sieve with the back of a spoon, but do not attempt to push all the solids through the sieve.

With the lamb racks meat-side up, brush the top of the racks with the honey mixture. Place the meat under the broiler for about 3 minutes, or until the top of the racks are nicely caramelized. Cut each rack into 8 chops and arrange 4 on each of 4 plates. Pour the liquid from the roasting pan over, garnish with watercress sprigs, and serve.

Makes 4 servings

Pears with Calvados
Poires au Calvados

4 ripe pears
2 tablespoons unsalted butter
½ cup sugar
4 tablespoons Calvados
2 eggs
Pinch of ground cinnamon
Salt to taste
1 tablespoon all-purpose flour
¾ cup heavy (whipping) cream

Preheat the oven to 350°F. Lightly butter a dish or ovenproof casserole just large enough to hold the pears.

Peel and core the pears. Halve them lengthwise and cut each half into 4 wedges. In a sauté pan or skillet, melt the butter over medium heat and add the pears. Sprinkle them with ¼ cup of the sugar and sauté the pears until they are lightly caramelized. Add 2 tablespoons of the Calvados, let it warm, and ignite with a match; shake the pan until the flames subside. Place the pears and Calvados mixture in the prepared dish.

In a medium bowl, whisk together the eggs and the remaining ¼ cup sugar until the eggs are frothy and pale in color. Add the cinnamon, salt, and flour. Slowly stir in the cream and the remaining 2 tablespoons of the Calvados. Pour this mixture over the pears. Bake in the preheated oven for 35 minutes, or until the top is lightly golden brown. Serve warm.

Makes 4 servings

Mark's Restaurant offers extraordinary food in a setting that has been compared to a chic London dining club. Since its opening in 1989, the restaurant has been one of New York's most applauded hotel restaurants. Its superb French-inspired *cuisine moderne* is complemented by a wine list that has won the *Wine Spectator's* Award of Excellence. Mark's offers breakfast, lunch, afternoon tea, and a leisurely Sunday brunch. The restaurant has also become known for its Vintners' Dinners, which showcase the selections of a notable wine maker each month, coupled with a special three-course menu created by chef Erik Maillard.

Located in the intimate and luxurious Mark Hotel, which underwent a $35 million renovation in 1989, Mark's is in the heart of the Upper East Side, just steps away from the Metropolitan Museum of Art and Central Park.

Mark's Restaurant

THE MENU
Mark's Restaurant

Melon Soup with Cured Cucumbers

Salmon and Sea-Scallop Sausages

Honey-glazed Roasted Rack of Lamb

Spicy Fig Stew with Honey-Yogurt Sauce

Serves Four

Melon Soup with Cured Cucumbers

1 small honeydew melon
2 small cantaloupes
1½ tablespoons fresh lemon juice, or to taste
Salt and freshly ground white pepper to taste
1 small cucumber
1 cup coarse salt
1 small tomato, peeled, seeded, and diced
⅓ cup minced fresh cilantro

Peel the honeydew melon and cantaloupes, scoop out the seeds, and cut the fruit into cubes. In a blender or food processor, purée the melon cubes with the lemon juice. Strain the purée through a fine-meshed sieve into a large bowl and season with salt and pepper. Cover and chill in the refrigerator for 1 or 2 hours.

Peel the cucumber and cut it in half lengthwise. With a spoon, scrape out the seeds and discard them. Sprinkle the cucumber generously with the coarse salt, place in a sieve or colander, and drain for 15 to 20 minutes. Rinse the cucumber under cold water and drain well.

To serve, cut the cucumber into thin slices. Divide the cucumber slices among 4 shallow soup bowls, arranging them in the center of each bowl. Ladle in the chilled soup, sprinkle with the diced tomato and cilantro, and serve.

Makes 4 servings

Mark's Restaurant

Salmon and Sea Scallop Sausages

Caul fat is a lacelike membrane from the belly of the pig and is used as a covering for small sausages. Order it from a specialty butcher shop.

Two 4-ounce salmon fillets, plus 3 ounces salmon, diced
15 large spinach leaves, stemmed
4 sea scallops, diced
1½ tablespoons minced fresh tarragon
3½ tablespoons minced fresh parsley
Salt and freshly ground pepper to taste
1 lime wedge
8 ounces caul fat

Garnish
12 small red potatoes, trimmed to olive shapes
8 asparagus stalks
8 baby leeks, white part only
1 tablespoon butter

½ cup mild olive oil
1 tablespoon butter
Beurre Nantais (recipe follows)
¼ cup minced fresh chives

Cover the salmon fillets with plastic wrap and chill in the freezer until nearly frozen, about 2 hours. Cut each fillet into 8 diagonal slices. Pound the slices between 2 sheets of waxed paper to make them thinner; set aside.

Steam the spinach over boiling water in a covered pan until wilted, 2 or 3 minutes. Rinse the leaves in cold water, drain, and set aside. In a large bowl, stir together the diced scallops, diced salmon, and minced tarragon and parsley. Season with salt, pepper, and a squeeze of lime, and set aside.

On a work surface, spread out the caul fat and cut it into a 20-inch square. Cover the caul fat with the spinach. Place the pounded salmon slices on top of

Mark's Restaurant

the spinach leaves in an even layer and lightly season with salt and pepper. Place the diced scallops and salmon mixture in a line across one end of the square. Carefully roll up the caul fat and tie the sausage at each end with cotton string. (The sausage should be firm but not too hard.)

To make the garnish: Blanch each of the vegetables in boiling salted water, about 8 minutes for the potatoes and 6 minutes for the asparagus and leeks; drain. Rinse the asparagus and leeks under cold water; drain again, set aside, and keep warm. Pat the potatoes dry with paper towels. In a small sauté pan or skillet, melt the butter and sauté the potatoes over medium heat for several minutes until golden brown on all sides; remove from the pan with a slotted spoon, set aside, and keep warm.

In a large sauté pan or skillet, heat the olive oil and butter over medium heat and sauté the sausage for 6 minutes for medium rare and 8 minutes for medium. Remove from the pan and cut the sausage into slices.

Arrange the baby leeks and asparagus in the center of each of 4 appetizer plates. Top and surround the vegetables with the sausage slices. Spoon some of the warm beurre nantais around the sausage slices, sprinkle the minced chives over all, and serve.

Makes 1 large sausage; serves 4

Beurre Nantais

1 cup dry white wine
3 shallots, minced
1 tablespoon white wine vinegar
1 cup (2 sticks) butter, cut into 16 pieces
Salt and freshly ground pepper to taste

In a large saucepan over high heat, combine the wine, shallots, and vinegar and cook until the liquid has almost all evaporated, 1 to 2 minutes. Reduce the heat to low and whisk in the butter 1 piece at a time; the sauce will thicken and emulsify. Season to taste with salt and pepper and keep warm over barely tepid water.

Makes about 1 cup

Mark's Restaurant

Honey-glazed Roasted Rack of Lamb

4 racks of lamb (4 chops each)

2 cups honey

1½ teaspoons ground cumin

1 teaspoon ground coriander

½ teaspoon ground allspice

½ teaspoon ground cinnamon

½ teaspoon ground nutmeg

¼ teaspoon ground white pepper

Pinch of cayenne pepper

1 cup water

2 tablespoons minced onion

1 teaspoon minced fresh thyme

Salt to taste

1 teaspoon white wine vinegar

20 asparagus spears, peeled and blanched for 6 minutes

2 tomatoes, peeled, seeded, and cut into eighths

8 sun-dried tomatoes, sliced

12 black olives, pitted and quartered

12 green olives, pitted, quartered, and blanched

1 to 2 tablespoons olive oil

Leaves and flowers from 3 fresh lavender stems

Have your butcher remove most of the fat and the chine (backbone) from the racks, French cut the rib bones, and give you the fat, bones, and trimmings.

Preheat the oven to 400°F. In a small bowl, stir together the honey, cumin, coriander, allspice, cinnamon, nutmeg, white pepper, and cayenne pepper; set aside.

In a large sauté pan or skillet, render some of the reserved lamb fat and brown the bones and trimmings over medium heat. Pour off the fat. Pour in a large spoonful of the honey mixture and the water. Cook over medium heat, stirring to scrape up the browned bits on the bottom of the pan, until the liquid is slightly reduced, about 5 minutes. Strain through a fine-meshed sieve and discard the bones and trimmings. Return to the pan and add the onion, thyme, and salt. Cook over medium heat until reduced to a sauce. Stir in the vinegar and adjust the seasoning; set aside.

Sprinkle the racks with salt. Place them in a roasting pan and bake in the preheated oven for 12 minutes. Spread the spiced honey evenly over the racks and bake for 13 more minutes for medium rare.

Meanwhile, in a large bowl, toss together the asparagus, fresh and dried tomatoes, black and green olives, olive oil, and minced lavender.

To serve, arrange the vegetables in the center of each plate. Cut each rack of lamb into 4 chops and arrange the chops against the vegetables. Spoon the sauce around the chops and serve.

Makes 4 servings

Mark's Restaurant

Spicy Fig Stew with Honey-Yogurt Sauce

This stew serves 6, but leftovers store well. To serve 4, use 1½ oranges and 4 fresh figs for the garnish and two thirds of the yogurt sauce.

1½ pounds dried figs
2 cinnamon sticks
1 teaspoon coriander seeds
½ teaspoon cumin seeds
3 cloves
1 teaspoon peppercorns
2 star anise
½ teaspoon fennel seeds
1 fresh bay leaf, or ½ dried bay leaf
1 tablespoon honey, plus more to taste
1 tablespoon balsamic vinegar, plus more to taste
½ cup raisins
Salt to taste
2 oranges
2 cups plain yogurt
6 fresh figs
1 tablespoon minced fresh mint

Using a sharp knife, cut the dried figs in half lengthwise, including the stem. Place the figs in a medium saucepan. Place the cinnamon sticks, cumin seeds, cloves, peppercorns, star anise, and fennel seeds on a wooden board. Use a rolling pin to crack the spices. Place all the cracked spices plus the whole or half bay leaf on a square of cheesecloth, tie into a bag with cotton string, and add the bag to the figs. Add 1 tablespoon honey, 1 tablespoon balsamic vinegar, and the raisins to the saucepan. Add water to cover and simmer over low heat until the figs are soft yet retain a bit of their shape. Adjust the seasonings with more vinegar and honey or salt if necessary; set aside.

In a small bowl, mix the yogurt with honey to taste. Peel the oranges and cut them in thin slices, then in half. Cut off the stems of the fresh figs and cut each fig into 8 wedges.

Spoon some of the stew into the center of each of 6 shallow soup bowls and spoon the yogurt sauce around the edges. Place the orange slices on top of the stew. Garnish with wedges of figs, sprinkle with mint, and serve.

Makes 6 servings

PALIO

Located in the immense Equitable Center in midtown Manhattan, Palio opened its doors in 1986. Full-course dinners are enjoyed in the elegant contemporary second-floor dining room, which is entered by a private elevator. Chef Hans Kaufmann hails from Merano in northern Italy, and his authentic Italian food pairs invention with tradition. Kaufmann carries on the extremely high standards of his mentor, chef Andrea Hellrigl, who contributed so much to Palio's original success. Delectable cuisine, a world-class wine list, impeccable service, and dazzling decor combine to make dining at Palio a marvelous sensory experience.

Palio is managed by proprietor Maria Pia Hellrigl. The restaurant's dramatic ground-level bar is dominated by Sandro Chia's mural of the *Palio* of Siena, an eight-hundred-year-old event honoring the Assumption of the Virgin, in which the palio, a banner of precious cloth, is awarded to the victors of a wild and reckless horse race. The colorful 124-foot-long mural encircles the bar.

Balsamic vinegar is chef Kaufmann's theme for the following dinner, and it plays a role in each course.

THE MENU
Palio

Lightly Smoked Scallops with a Potato Dressing

Lobster Maccheroni with Balsamic Vinegar

Poached Beef with Steamed Vegetables in Pomegranate-Balsamic Sauce

Balsamic Strawberries and Yogurt Soup

Serves Four

Lightly Smoked Scallops with a Potato Dressing

12 sea scallops (about 1 ounce each)
Salt to taste
1 cup dry white wine
1 garlic clove
1 bay leaf
2 to 3 fresh basil leaves
5 cups water
About ½ cup mixed herbs and citrus peel such as fresh rosemary sprigs,
    dried sage sprigs, bay leaves, and orange peel

Potato Dressing
One 6-ounce Idaho potato, peeled and cut into pieces
6 tablespoons olive oil
2 shallots, minced
1 tablespoon white wine vinegar
Salt and freshly ground pepper to taste
About 1 cup chicken stock (see page 202) or canned low-salt chicken broth

Baby greens such as frisée, mâche, and red leaf lettuce
Balsamic Sauce (see page 143) for garnish

Sprinkle the scallops lightly with salt. To a large saucepan or stockpot, add
the wine, garlic clove, bay leaf, basil leaves, water, and salt to taste; bring to a
boil. When the liquid is boiling, add the scallops, lower the heat to medium, and
poach the scallops for 4 to 6 minutes. Using a slotted spoon, remove the scallops
and let cool.

In a smoker or charcoal grill, burn hardwood (such as hickory) or hardwood
charcoal down to coals covered with gray ash (if using a grill, place the wood or
charcoal on one side of the fuel bed). Soak the rosemary, dry sage, bay leaves,
and orange peel in water for about 30 minutes. Drain the herbs and peel and

place them on top of the coals. Place the scallops in the smoker, or on the cooking grate of the grill on the side opposite the coals. Cover the smoker or grill and smoke the scallops for 20 minutes. Remove the scallops from the smoker or grill and slice them into thirds crosswise.

While the scallops are smoking, make the potato dressing: In a large pot of boiling salted water, cook the potato until very tender when pierced with a knife, about 15 minutes; drain and set aside. In a small sauté pan or skillet, heat the olive oil over medium heat and sauté the shallots for 2 minutes. Place the potato, shallots, vinegar, salt, and pepper in a blender or food processor and purée, adding enough stock or broth to make a smooth sauce; set aside.

To serve, form a circle with 9 overlapping scallop slices in the center of each of 4 plates. In the center of each circle, place the baby greens. Drop 3 spoonfuls of potato dressing near the rim of the plate where the points of a triangle would be. Sprinkle dots of balsamic sauce around the rim of the plate between the spoonfuls of potato dressing.

Makes 4 servings

Palio

Balsamic Sauce

2 pounds small veal bones, cut into pieces
1 cup olive oil
4 cups mixed diced leeks, carrots, celery, onions, and mushrooms
Minced fresh rosemary and thyme to taste
4 garlic cloves
Freshly ground pepper to taste
1 bottle dry red wine (not too strong or acidic)
¼ cup balsamic vinegar, plus more to taste
½ gallon water

Preheat the oven to 450°F. Place the bones in a roasting pan, coat them with the olive oil, and roast them for 30 minutes, or until they are a deep brown. Add the diced vegetables, herbs, garlic, and pepper, and continue roasting for another 30 minutes, stirring frequently. Pour the fat out of the roasting pan. Pour in about one third of the red wine and one third of the balsamic vinegar, and cook over medium-high heat until the liquid has almost evaporated. Repeat twice. Add the water and bring to a boil. Place the pan in the oven at 400°F for 2 hours. Strain through a sieve into a large saucepan (discard the solids) and boil to reduce the liquid again until there are 2 cups of sauce left. Add a little fresh balsamic vinegar to enhance the taste.

Makes 2 cups

Palio

Lobster Maccheroni with Balsamic Vinegar

One 2-pound lobster
8 ounces maccheroni
½ cup (1 stick) butter
1½ teaspoons balsamic vinegar, preferably 12 years old, or
   Balsamic Sauce (page 143)
1½ teaspoons veal glaze (see page 207)

Kill the lobster by inserting a knife at the point where the body meets the tail. Plunge the lobster into a pot of rapidly boiling salted water, return it to boiling, and cook for 8 minutes. Remove the lobster from the boiling water with a slotted spoon and let cool. Shell the lobster and remove all the meat. Cut the meat into large cubes and refrigerate. (The lobster can be cooked 1 day in advance.)

In a large pot of boiling salted water, cook the maccheroni for 8 to 10 minutes, or until al dente. Drain, reserving 2 tablespoons of the water.

In a large sauté pan or skillet, melt the butter over medium heat. Stir in the 2 tablespoons of water from the maccheroni, the cubes of lobster meat, and the cooked maccheroni; mix well. Divide the lobster maccheroni evenly among 4 plates.

In a small saucepan over medium heat, stir together the balsamic vinegar or sauce and veal glaze until warmed. Spoon this sauce around the maccheroni and serve at once.

Makes 4 servings

Poached Beef with Steamed Vegetables in Pomegranate-Balsamic Sauce

2½ pounds beef tenderloin, well trimmed

8 cups strong beef stock (see page 201) or canned low-salt beef broth,
   or enough to cover the beef in a casserole

16 baby carrots, peeled

2 potatoes, peeled and cut into julienne

1 celery stalk, cut into julienne

1 small zucchini, cut into julienne

8 green onions, white part only

Pomegranate-Balsamic Sauce

⅓ cup virgin olive oil

⅓ cup reduced veal stock (see page 207)

2 tablespoons balsamic vinegar or Balsamic Sauce (page 143)

¼ cup capers, drained

2 tablespoons pine nuts

⅓ cup pomegranate seeds

2 tablespoons dried currents, plumped in warm tea for 15 minutes
   and drained

Salt and freshly ground pepper to taste

Place the beef tenderloin in a Dutch oven or heatproof casserole just large enough to hold it and cover the meat with the beef stock or broth. Bring to a boil and reduce heat to low. Cover and simmer for approximately 15 minutes for rare beef, or a bit longer if more well-done meat is desired.

While the beef is cooking, steam the carrots, potatoes, celery, zucchini, and green onions in a large saucepan with ½ inch of boiling salted water for 2 to 3 minutes, or until tender. Remove from heat and drain.

To make the sauce: In a small bowl, combine the olive oil, veal stock, balsamic vinegar or sauce, capers, pine nuts, pomegranate seeds, and plumped currants. Season with salt and pepper.

To serve, place the steamed vegetables on 4 individual plates. Cut the beef into ½-inch-thick slices and arrange over a bed of the steamed vegetables. Generously spoon the sauce over the meat.

Makes 4 servings

Balsamic Strawberries and Yogurt Soup

2½ cups fresh strawberries, hulled
1½ cups sugar
5 tablespoons balsamic vinegar or Balsamic Sauce (page 143)
Grated zest of 1 orange
Grated zest of 1 lemon
1 teaspoon Grand Marnier
3 cups plain yogurt
4 fresh mint sprigs for garnish

In a food processor or blender, purée 1 cup of the strawberries, ½ cup of the sugar, 3 tablespoons of the vinegar, half of the orange zest, and half of the lemon zest. Strain the puree through a sieve into a bowl. Stir in the remaining orange and lemon zest, the Grand Marnier, and yogurt. Whisk the finished soup until smooth; cover with plastic wrap and chill in the refrigerator.

Meanwhile, in a large bowl, place the remaining 1 cup sugar with the remaining 2 tablespoons balsamic vinegar and stir until well mixed. Stir the remaining 1½ cups strawberries with the sugar and balsamic vinegar mixture. Marinate for 1 to 2 hours.

Just before serving, place 4 or 5 marinated strawberries into each of 4 shallow soup bowls. Stir the chilled soup and ladle about ¾ cup of it over the strawberries. Using a teaspoon, take some the juice from the marinated strawberries and drizzle a design in the soup. Garnish with a fresh mint sprig and serve.

Makes 4 servings

Palio

Parioli Romanissimo

Diners come to Parioli Romanissimo for inspired Italian dining in the grand tradition. The restaurant is set in a beautiful old town house on the Upper East Side, just a short walk from the Metropolitan Museum of Art. Proprietor Rubrio Rossi's passions are good food and elegant surroundings. Trained as an architect, he installed a glass-enclosed garden atrium at the back of the restaurant and decorated the main dining room in an elegant and classic style that befits a venerable building. Parioli Romanissimo's menu offers glorious pastas, generously portioned main courses, a cheese course offering choices from forty or more cheeses, and luscious desserts. Attentive captains and waiters bring warmth and enthusiasm to their work. The restaurant's superb menu, world-class wine list, attentive service, and decor combine to make dining here an extraordinary experience.

Parioli Romanissimo

THE MENU

Parioli Romanissimo

Tagliolini with White Truffles

Rack of Veal with Rosemary

Devilish Potatoes

Coffee Granita

Serves Four

Tagliolini with White Truffles
Tagliolini al Tartufo Bianco

1 cup (2 sticks) unsalted butter, at room temperature

2 ounces white truffles, minced, plus white truffle slices for garnish

6 tablespoons freshly grated Parmesan cheese

1 pound fresh tagliolini

1 cup heavy (whipping) cream

In a blender or food processor, combine the butter, white truffles, and Parmesan cheese; process until smooth and creamy, and set aside.

In a large stockpot, bring a large amount of salted water to a boil. Stir in the tagliolini, return the water to a boil, and cook for 2 to 3 minutes, or until al dente; drain. In a large skillet add the truffle mixture, cooked pasta, and cream; mix well and heat through. Arrange the pasta on 4 serving plates and top with a generous amount of white truffle slices.

Makes 4 servings

Rack of Veal with Rosemary
Carre di Vitello al Rosmarino

1 rack of veal (4 double veal chops, uncut)
Olive oil for coating
Salt and freshly ground pepper to taste
2 tablespoons each fresh thyme and rosemary leaves
4 bacon strips
4 garlic cloves, unpeeled
4 cups dry white wine
2 cups beef stock (see page 201) or canned low-salt beef broth

Preheat the oven to 400°F. Place the rack in a roasting pan and coat with olive oil. Sprinkle with salt, pepper, thyme, and rosemary. Add the bacon and garlic. Roast for 20 minutes on one side, turn, and roast for another 20 minutes. Pour off the fat, add the wine and stock or broth, and bake for 30 minutes more, basting frequently. Remove the rack from the pan. Strain the pan juices through a fine-meshed sieve. Pour the juices over the veal rack and serve immediately.

Makes 4 servings

Devilish Potatoes
Patate al Diavolicchio

¼ cup olive oil
6 red potatoes, peeled and thinly sliced
½ tablespoon minced garlic
1 tablespoon butter
Dried red pepper flakes to taste
Salt and minced fresh parsley to taste

In a large sauté pan or skillet, heat the olive oil over high heat, add the potatoes, and cook until lightly browned and tender, about 15 minutes. Add the garlic, butter, and red pepper flakes, and cook a few minutes more. Transfer the potatoes to a serving dish and sprinkle with salt and minced parsley.

Makes 4 servings

Parioli Romanissimo

Coffee Granita
Granita di Caffè

4 cups cold brewed espresso
¾ cup superfine sugar

    In a large bowl, stir together the espresso and sugar. Place the bowl in the freezer for about 1 hour. Remove from the freezer and stir gently. Return the bowl to the freezer and stir every 30 minutes until the espresso is the texture of crushed ice, about 3 hours. (Do not allow it to freeze completely.) Serve the granita in tall champagne glasses.

Makes 4 servings

Parioli Romanissimo

PETROSSIAN
RESTAURANT

Opened in 1984, Petrossian Restaurant is housed in the historic Alwyn Court Building on Manhattan's West Side, just a block from Central Park. It serves a French-inspired contemporary menu featuring the caviars, smoked fish, and foie gras delicacies for which the Petrossian company is known throughout the world.

A family business, Petrossian was founded in Paris in the 1920s by two brothers, Melkoum and Moucheg Petrossian. They introduced caviar to the Parisian public and were among the first to trade with the newly formed USSR. For seventy years, the Petrossian family maintained a privileged relationship with the Russians, being the first to hand-pick their caviar directly from the choicest catches of the Caspian Sea. Today, Petrossian, under the direction of owner Armen Petrossian, is the largest buyer and importer of Russian caviar to France, the United States, and Canada.

Executive chef Joseph Pace's varied and imaginative menus for brunch, lunch, and dinner are offered in the beautiful Ion Oroveanu–designed restaurant. A la carte or prix-fixe dining can be enjoyed at the Art Deco–style mirrored bar, or at the restaurant's linen-covered tables where diners are pampered by formal service. Sharing space with the restaurant is the Delicacies Boutique, which carries the complete line of Petrossian products.

THE MENU

Petrossian

Russian Sevruga Caviar with Blini and Crème Fraîche

*Salad of Smoked Brook Trout with Cured Horseradish
and Lemon Dressing*

*Maine Lobster Fricassee with Root Vegetables
on a Bed of Potato Purée*

New England Spice Cake with Cinnamon Ice Cream

Serves Four

Russian Sevruga Caviar with Blini and Crème Fraîche

1 package active dried yeast
3½ cups warm milk (105° to 115°F)
2¾ cups all-purpose flour
4 eggs, separated
Pinch of salt
6 tablespoons whipped cream
2 tablespoons butter
¾ cup crème fraîche (see page 203)
About 4 ounces fresh Russian Sevruga caviar

In a large bowl, whisk together the yeast, 2¼ cups of the warm milk, and ½ cup of the flour. Cover and let sit in a warm place for 2 hours.

In a large bowl, beat the egg whites with the salt until stiff peaks form; set aside. Beat the egg yolks lightly, then whisk them into the yeast mixture with the remaining 1¼ cups warm milk. Whisk in the remaining 2¼ cups flour by thirds. Fold in the beaten egg whites, salt, and whipped cream just until blended. Cover and let rise at room temperature for 35 minutes.

Preheat the oven to 200°F. In a blini pan about 3½ inches in diameter, melt ½ teaspoon of the butter over medium heat and tilt to coat the bottom. Pour in ⅓ cup of the blini batter. Tilt the pan to coat the bottom completely and cook the pancake until bubbles appear evenly on the surface and the edges are dry; turn and cook until browned on the second side. Place in the preheated oven. Repeat until all the batter has been used up. Serve the blini warm, topping each one with 1 tablespoon of crème fraîche and a little of the caviar.

Makes about 12 blini, or 4 appetizer servings

Salad of Smoked Brook Trout with Cured Horseradish and Lemon Dressing

Start this recipe 2 days before serving.

1 tablespoon freshly grated horseradish
½ cup crème fraîche (see page 203)
3 tablespoons fresh lemon juice
Pinch of salt
1 teaspoon coriander seeds
1 teaspoon mustard seeds
4 Petrossian smoked trout, skinned, boned (reserve the bones), and flaked
1 cup mixed baby greens
2 tablespoons minced fresh chives
Salt and freshly ground pepper to taste

Place the horseradish in a small ceramic bowl and add 2 tablespoons of the lemon juice and the salt. Cover and let sit at room temperature for 2 days.

Place the crème fraîche in a sieve lined with muslin, place over a bowl, cover, and drain in the refrigerator for 12 hours.

The day of serving, make the dressing: In a small nonaluminum saucepan, stir the coriander and mustard seeds constantly over low heat until the seeds are fragrant. Add the reserved fish bones and enough water to cover by half. Bring to a simmer, then remove from heat. Let steep until cool, then strain though a fine-meshed sieve lined with muslin. Whisk this liquid with the remaining 1 tablespoon lemon juice, the drained crème fraîche, and cured horseradish to taste.

Place the greens in a salad bowl and add the flaked trout, chives, and some of the dressing. Toss until the salad is lightly coated. Season with salt and pepper and serve on cold salad plates.

Makes 4 servings

Maine Lobster Fricassee with Root Vegetables on a Bed of Potato Purée

Mushroom Sauce

2 pounds white mushrooms

2 quarts water

1 cup (2 sticks) butter

2 ounces (⅔ cup) small whole chanterelles

Salt to taste

4 small heads fennel, sliced

4 ounces (about 2 cups) Brussels sprouts, quartered

2 cups chicken stock (see page 202) or canned low-salt chicken broth

1 bunch baby carrots

1 bunch baby turnips

Potato Purée

2 quarts water

¼ cup salt, plus more to taste

1 pound potatoes, peeled and chopped

1 cup (2 sticks) unsalted butter, cut into pieces and at room temperature

¼ cup milk, warmed

Beurre Blanc

6 tablespoons *each* white wine vinegar and dry white wine

3 large shallots, minced

5 white peppercorns, crushed

2 cups (4 sticks) cold butter, cut into tablespoon-sized pieces

Salt to taste, if needed

4 live Maine lobsters, 1¼ pounds each (females, if possible)

4 ounces sugar snap peas, shelled (reserve pods)

½ tablespoon *each* minced fresh tarragon, parsley, and chives

Petrossian

Foie Gras Sauce

4 ounces Petrossian duck foie gras

2 tablespoons chicken stock (see page 202) or canned low-salt chicken
  broth, heated

Salt and freshly ground pepper to taste

1 bunch fresh chervil for garnish

To make the mushroom sauce: Put the white mushrooms in a large pot with
the water and simmer slowly until reduced to about 2 cups. Fill the pot again
with more cold water and cook to reduce again. Strain out the mushrooms and
simmer to reduce the remaining liquid until the mushroom flavor is strong and
the color is rich. You should have about ½ cup of liquid. Strain through cheesecloth and set aside.

In a heavy pot, melt 4 tablespoons of the butter over low heat, add the
chanterelles and a generous amount of salt, and cook slowly until the mushrooms release and reabsorb their juices and become very succulent. Set aside.

Blanch the fennel slices and quartered Brussels sprouts separately in boiling salted water for 3 minutes. Rinse in cold water, drain, and set aside.

Place 1 cup of the stock or broth, 4 tablespoons of the butter, the salt, carrots,
and turnips in a medium sauté pan or skillet. Bring to a simmer, partially cover,
and cook slowly to reduce the stock or broth until the vegetables are glazed but
still firm. Remove from heat, cover the pan, and place it in the refrigerator.

To make the potato purée: Place the water and ¼ cup salt in a large stockpot.
Add the potatoes, bring to a boil, then reduce the heat to a simmer. Cook for
about 15 minutes, or until the potatoes are tender. Drain and push the potatoes
through a food mill or ricer, or mash with a potato masher (do not use a food
processor). Slowly stir in the butter and milk until the potatoes are very smooth
but still somewhat stiff. (You may need to use more or less butter and milk to gain
the correct consistency.) Season to taste and cover with plastic wrap touching the
surface of the purée to keep it from forming a crust. Place in a very low oven
until ready to serve. This can be done up to 1 hour before serving.

Petrossian

To make the beurre blanc: Combine the vinegar, wine, shallots, and peppercorns in a heavy pan and cook over medium heat to reduce to a thick glaze. Whisk in a little of the butter at a time over low heat until all the butter has been absorbed and the sauce has thickened. Add salt if necessary. Keep warm over barely tepid water.

To cook the lobsters: Kill the lobsters by inserting a knife in the back of the shell where the chest and tail meet. Then, using a towel to protect your hands, separate each lobster into 4 pieces. Remove the large claw and the small claw, and separate the body from the tail by twisting the lobster in your hands. Clean the tail piece of any roe or tomalley that remains inside the top end. Let sit at room temperature for 30 minutes.

Bring a large pot of unsalted water to a boil. When the water is at a rolling boil, drop the small claws in for 1 minute. Remove with a slotted spoon. Allow the water to come back to a full boil and repeat to cook the large claws for 1½ minutes and the tails for 1¼ minutes.

Let the meat cool in the shells and, using a pair of needle-nose pliers, remove the shells carefully from the claws. Snip the ends off each claw, loosen the pincer, and slide the shell off the meat. Snip along the top of the shell with the pliers, pulling the shell back and off, and removing the flesh in one piece if possible. For the tails, remove each tailfin piece at the back by prying it back and forth until it snaps off. Then crack the shell between your hands and spread it away from the meat until the shell pops out. Reserve the claws, knuckles and tails. (The lobster will be cut into bite-sized pieces for serving, so do not worry if the flesh is not removed whole from the shell.) Slice the tails in half lengthwise and remove the intestine and remaining roe.

Preheat the oven to 325°F. Place the lobster pieces in a single layer in a heavy pan and add warm beurre blanc to cover. Place in the oven for about 10 minutes. Meanwhile, cook the mushroom sauce over medium heat until it is reduced to a thick syrup.

Place the shelled snap peas and pods in ½ cup of the stock or broth in a small saucepan, season, and cook over low heat for 5 minutes, or until crisp-tender; set aside. Place the blanched vegetables and mushrooms in another pan with 4 teaspoons of the beurre blanc, the remaining ½ cup of the stock or broth, and the minced herbs. Season and warm over low heat. Strain the peas and add to the blanched vegetables; set aside and keep warm.

To make the foie gras sauce: Break up the foie gras into small chunks. Place it in a blender, add the hot stock or broth, and blend at high speed until smooth. Season to taste. Strain and set aside.

Spoon a circle of potato purée into the center of each dinner plate. Remove the lobster from the beurre blanc, cut the tails into bite-sized pieces, and nestle them in the bed of potato. Spoon the vegetables carefully over the lobster. Place the claws on top of the vegetables. Spoon the reduced mushroom juice around the fricassee until it just coats the plate, then spoon a light drizzle of foie gras sauce on top. Garnish with sprigs of chervil and serve.

Makes 4 servings

New England Spice Cake with Cinnamon Ice Cream

¼ cup milk
½ cup egg whites (about 3 whites)
1½ cups plus 2 tablespoons cake flour
¾ cup plus 1 tablespoon sugar
¾ teaspoon ground cinnamon
½ teaspoon ground cloves
⅛ teaspoon ground nutmeg
⅛ teaspoon ground coriander
1 teaspoon baking powder
½ teaspoon salt
1 teaspoon unsweetened cocoa powder
¾ cup (1½ sticks) plus 3 tablespoons unsalted butter at
   room temperature
Cinnamon Ice Cream (recipe follows)

In a small bowl, lightly stir together the milk and egg whites. Sift the cinnamon, cloves, nutmeg, coriander, baking powder, salt, and cocoa powder, flour, sugar into a large mixer bowl. On low speed, add the butter and half of the egg white mixture. Increase the speed to medium and beat for 1 minute. Scrape down the sides and gradually add the remaining egg white mixture in 2 batches, beating for 20 seconds after each addition. Cover and refrigerate for 1 hour.

Preheat the oven to 300°F and butter four 4-inch fluted molds with removable bottoms. Pour the batter into the molds and bake in the preheated oven for 15 minutes, or until a toothpick inserted in the center of each mold comes out clean. Let cool and remove from the pans.

Makes 4 cakes

Cinnamon Ice Cream

2 cups milk
2 cinnamon sticks, broken into pieces
6 egg yolks
¾ cup sugar
¾ teaspoon ground cinnamon
1 cup heavy (whipping) cream

In a medium saucepan, combine the milk and cinnamon sticks. Bring just to a boil over high heat. Remove from heat and set aside.

In a medium bowl, beat the yolks and sugar together until thick and pale in color. Mix in the ground cinnamon. Remove the cinnamon sticks from the hot milk with a slotted spoon, blend the cinnamon sticks in a blender for 1 minute, and pour them back into the saucepan. Whisk one third of the hot milk into the yolk mixture. Pour that mixture back into the saucepan and place over medium heat. Stir constantly with a wooden spoon until the mixture thickens to a creamy consistency; do not let it boil. Remove the pan from heat and immediately stir in the cream to stop the cooking. Strain the mixture through a fine-meshed sieve and let cool. Cover and chill for several hours or overnight.

Freeze in an ice cream machine according to the manufacturer's instructions. Remove from the machine, place in a plastic container, and freeze for 1 hour before serving.

Makes about 2 quarts

Opened in 1978, Primavera reflects the talent and gracious personality of proprietor Nicola Civetta. Every evening, Civetta greets the guests at his popular Upper East Side restaurant with enthusiasm and sincerity, making them feel at home. The menu of northern Italian cuisine is based on ingredients of superb quality, presented with a sense of balance and style. The dining room is wood paneled, softly upholstered, and as cozy as a private club. Primavera is an oasis of friendly, comfortable luxury and fine food.

Primavera

THE MENU
Primavera

Aromatic Scampi

Risotto with Vegetables

Veal with Balsamic Vinegar

Tiramisù

Serves Six

Aromatic Scampi
Scampi Aromatici

Flour, salt, and freshly ground pepper for dredging
1¾ pounds scampi or large shrimp, peeled and deveined
¼ cup olive oil
4 tablespoons butter
¾ cup dry white wine
3 tablespoons capers, drained
Juice of ½ lemon, or more to taste
¼ cup finely chopped fresh tomatoes
7 tablespoons vegetable broth
Minced fresh parsley for garnish

In a shallow dish, combine the flour, salt, and pepper, and dredge the scampi or shrimp in the flour mixture. In a large sauté pan or skillet, heat the olive oil and butter over medium heat and sauté the scampi or shrimp for 3 to 4 minutes, or until they turn pink. Add the wine, bring to a boil, and cook until the wine evaporates. Remove the scampi from the pan and place on a hot serving dish. Cover to keep warm.

Add the capers, lemon juice, tomatoes, and vegetable broth to the pan and simmer for 5 to 10 minutes. Ladle the sauce over the scampi and sprinkle with the minced parsley. Serve warm.

Makes 6 servings

Primavera

Risotto with Vegetables
Risotto Primavera

This classic rice dish of northern Italy has been called "the porridge of the gods." Medium-grain rice is simmered and stirred constantly so that its flavorful cooking liquid is absorbed gradually.

2 tablespoons olive oil

1 onion, minced

4 slices prosciutto, minced

6 asparagus spears, chopped

1 cup chopped broccoli

1 cup chopped cauliflower

2 cups Arborio rice

1 cup dry white wine

8 cups veal stock (see page 207), chicken stock (see page 202), or canned
   low-salt chicken broth

6 mushrooms, sliced

3 ripe tomatoes, peeled, seeded, and chopped

2 zucchini, sliced

Salt and freshly ground pepper to taste

½ cup (1 stick) butter

1 cup (4 ounces) freshly grated Parmesan cheese

In a large, heavy saucepan, heat the olive oil over medium heat and sauté the onion and prosciutto until golden brown, about 5 minutes; set aside. Steam the asparagus, broccoli, and cauliflower separately over boiling water for 5 minutes each; set aside.

Add the rice to the pan with the onion and prosciutto, place over medium heat, and stir constantly for 2 minutes. Reduce heat to low and gradually stir in the wine and ½ cup of the stock or broth. When the liquid has been absorbed, gradually add 1 more cup of stock or broth while stirring. Add the steamed vegetables and the mushrooms, tomatoes, and zucchini. Gradually add the remaining stock or broth 1 cup at a time, stirring constantly, until all of the liquid has been absorbed and the rice is slightly creamy and just tender. Remove the pan from heat, season the risotto with salt and pepper, and stir in the butter and cheese. Serve warm.

Makes 6 servings

Primavera

Veal with Balsamic Vinegar
Vitello al'Aceto Balsamico

¼ cup olive oil
2 garlic cloves, chopped
2 small carrots, peeled and chopped
2 small celery stalks, chopped
One 2½-pound veal loin, boned and tied
1 cup dry white wine
½ cup balsamic vinegar
2 cups water
Salt and freshly ground pepper to taste

Preheat the oven to 325°F. In a Dutch oven or large heatproof casserole, heat the olive oil over medium heat and sauté the garlic, carrots, and celery for about 2 minutes; add the veal loin and brown lightly on all sides. Add the wine, vinegar, water, salt, and pepper. Cover the Dutch oven or casserole and bake for about 2 hours, or until tender.

Remove the veal to a carving board, discard the strings, and thinly slice the meat. Strain the pan juices into a saucepan over high heat, pressing juices out of the vegetables with the back of a spoon; discard the solids. Return the liquid to the pan, bring to a boil, and cook to reduce the liquid to a sauce. Ladle the juices over the sliced veal and serve.

Makes 6 servings

Primavera

Tiramisù

Tiramisù means "pick me up." This popular dessert is made with mascarpone, an Italian cheese similar to cream cheese.

36 ladyfingers
2 cups cold brewed espresso
¼ cup brandy
6 eggs, separated
6 tablespoons confectioners' sugar, sifted
1 pound mascarpone cheese at room temperature
8 ounces bittersweet or semisweet chocolate, grated

Arrange the ladyfingers in a single layer in a large, shallow dish. In a small bowl, stir together the espresso and brandy. Drizzle the coffee mixture over the ladyfingers and set them aside.

In a large bowl, beat the egg yolks and sugar until the mixture is thick and pale in color. In another large bowl, beat the egg whites until stiff peaks form. Gently fold the mascarpone into the yolk mixture, then fold the egg whites into the mascarpone mixture.

Arrange a layer of half of the soaked ladyfingers in the bottom of a shallow bowl or casserole. Cover with half of the mascarpone mixture and sprinkle with half of the grated chocolate. Add the remaining ladyfingers in a second layer and cover with the remaining mascarpone mixture. Top with the remaining grated chocolate. Cover with plastic wrap and chill in the refrigerator for at least 1 hour before serving.

Makes 6 servings

Tony May's

SANDOMENICO

Tony May opened San Domenico NY in 1988, and the restaurant still sets the standard for modern Italian cuisine in the United States. San Domenico has received three stars from the *New York Times* for its *alta cucina*, the cooking of Italy's aristocracy, and *Esquire* magazine has called San Domenico "one of the five best restaurants in the country."

Tony May has been at the forefront of efforts in the United States and Italy to foster a more complete understanding of Italian food and wine. He is the founder of the Gruppo Ristoratori Italiani, an association of restaurateurs, chefs, writers, and food purveyors dedicated to preserving and developing Italian cooking, and the author of *Italian Cuisine: Basic Cooking Techniques,* a textbook distributed exclusively to culinary arts schools throughout America. He travels frequently to Italy to gather new ideas for the restaurant's constantly evolving menu. Tony May's restaurant career has spanned four decades, and he is included in the *Who's Who of Cooking in America.*

San Domenico NY is located across from Central Park, just two blocks north of Carnegie Hall. The dining room's sleek lines, terra-cotta colors, burnished woods, and marble floors exemplify classic Italian style and give the restaurant a light and relaxing environment.

Executive chef Theo Schoenegger hails from Northern Italy and turns out dishes that visiting Italians rave about. Diners may order the chef's *menu de gustazione*, or dine quite reasonably from fixed-price lunch and dinner menus. San Domenico NY has an extensive collection of wines from Italy, California, and the Pacific Northwest.

San Domenico NY

THE MENU
San Domenico NY

*Pan-roasted Sweetbreads with Baby Greens
and Garlic-scented Sauce*

*Soft Egg-filled Ravioli with Hazelnut Butter
and White Truffles*

*Braised Guinea Hen with Savoy Cabbage
and Porcini Mushrooms*

Chocolate Polenta

Serves Four

Pan-roasted Sweetbreads with Baby Greens and Garlic-scented Sauce
Medaglioni di Animelle con Salsa all'Aglio

4 cups court bouillon (see page 203)

1 pound veal sweetbreads

Salt and freshly ground pepper to taste

1 cup white veal stock (see page 208), chicken stock (see page 202), or
   canned low-salt chicken broth

1 teaspoon fresh lemon juice

1 tomato, peeled, seeded, and diced

Corn oil for deep-frying

3 to 4 cups mixed baby greens such as mâche, arugula, mizuna,
   Bibb, and romaine

1 teaspoon garlic olive oil (see page 204)

In a large saucepan or stockpot over high heat, bring the court bouillon to a boil. Add the sweetbreads, reduce heat to low, and simmer for 10 minutes. Drain the sweetbreads and place them in a bowl of ice water; let sit for several minutes until they are cool. Using a sharp knife, trim away all the membranes. Cover the sweetbreads with plastic wrap and chill in the refrigerator for 1 or 2 hours.

Slice the sweetbreads into ½-inch-thick diagonal slices. Season the slices lightly with salt and pepper and dredge them in the flour one at a time, shaking off the excess flour; set aside.

In a small saucepan, combine the stock or broth, lemon juice, and tomato. Bring to a boil and cook to reduce to a syrupy consistency. Adjust the seasoning and keep warm.

To a large, heavy pot or deep-fryer, add corn oil to a depth of 2 inches and heat until almost smoking, about 375°F. Carefully add 3 to 4 slices of sweetbreads to the oil and cook until lightly browned, about 1 minute on each side. Using a slotted spoon, remove the slices from the oil, drain them on paper towels, and cover to keep warm until serving. Repeat until all the sweetbread slices are cooked.

San Domenico NY

Ladle a pool of warm sauce onto each 4 warmed plates and place a small mound of baby greens in the center of each plate. Arrange the fried sweetbread slices around the greens. Sprinkle with garlic olive oil and serve immediately.

Makes 4 servings

Soft Egg-filled Ravioli with Hazelnut Butter and White Truffles
Uovo in Raviolo con Burro Nocciola e Tartufi Bianchi

12 ounces spinach, stemmed

½ cup ricotta cheese

1 cup (4 ounces) freshly grated Parmesan cheese

1 egg

Ground nutmeg, salt, and ground white pepper to taste

Eight 6-inch rounds very thin pasta dough or 8 gyoza (round) noodle
    wrappers or wonton (square) noodle wrappers

4 egg yolks

2 egg whites

2 ounces white truffle, shaved with a truffle slicer or potato peeler

½ cup (1 stick) butter

Wash the spinach leaves and place them wet in a large saucepan. Place the pan over medium heat, cover, and cook for about 1 minute, or until wilted. Place the cooked spinach in a sieve and press it with the back or a large spoon to express as much liquid as possible. Chop the spinach finely. In a medium bowl, mix together the chopped spinach, ricotta, half of the Parmesan cheese, and the egg. Season to taste with nutmeg, salt, and pepper.

Place 4 pasta dough rounds or wrappers on waxed paper. Divide the ricotta and spinach mixture into 4 equal parts and place a mound of the mixture in the center of each round or square. Make an indentation in the center of each mound with the back of a tablespoon and place 1 egg yolk and 1 tablespoon egg white in the indentation. Sprinkle with salt and pepper. Brush the edges of the rounds or squares with cold water. Cover with the other 4 rounds or squares and press to seal, eliminating as much air as possible from the inside.

Bring a large pot of salted water to a boil. Meanwhile, in a small saucepan, melt the butter over medium heat and cook just until light brown; set aside and keep warm.

Reduce heat for the water to a gentle boil, add the ravioli, return the water to a boil, and cook for 2 minutes. Drain and place 1 raviolo on each of 4 warmed plates. Sprinkle with the truffles and remaining Parmesan cheese. Pour the warm browned butter over the ravioli and serve immediately.

Makes 4 servings

Braised Guinea Hen with Savoy Cabbage and Porcini Mushrooms
Faraona Brasata alle Verze con Funghi Porcini

One 3-pound guinea hen
Salt and freshly ground pepper to taste
3½ tablespoons butter
½ cup extra-virgin olive oil
5 garlic cloves
1 fresh rosemary sprig
10 ounces fresh porcini mushrooms, sliced
2 heads savoy or Napa cabbage, cored and coarsely chopped
4 cups chicken stock (see page 202) or canned low-salt chicken broth
Salt and freshly ground white pepper to taste

Preheat the oven to 300°F. Season the guinea hen with salt and pepper and tie the wings and drumsticks to the body with cotton string. Place the hen in a baking dish with the butter and 2 tablespoons of the olive oil. Bake in the pre-heated oven, turning frequently, for about 1 hour, or until the juices run clear when a thigh is pricked with a fork.

Meanwhile, in a large saucepan, heat the remaining 6 tablespoons olive oil, garlic cloves, and rosemary over medium heat until the oil is fragrant and warm to the touch; do not let the garlic brown. Let cool, then remove and discard the garlic cloves and rosemary.

Return the saucepan to medium heat and sauté the mushrooms for 2 to 3 minutes. Add the cabbage leaves and chicken stock or broth, reduce heat to low, and simmer for about 30 minutes. Add salt and pepper.

When the guinea hen is done, remove it from the pan and let sit for 10 minutes. Pour off the excess fat from the pan and add the cabbage and mushrooms. Cover the pan with aluminum foil and return it to the oven for about 10 minutes.

Cut the guinea hen into serving pieces and divide them among 4 heated plates. Garnish with the cabbage and porcini and serve immediately.

Makes 4 servings

San Domenico NY

Chocolate Polenta
Polenta Nera

1 ounce semisweet chocolate, chopped
¼ cup hazelnut paste
½ cup (1 stick) butter
⅓ cup polenta
1 cup milk
6 egg yolks, beaten
8 egg whites
½ cup sugar

Preheat the oven to 350°F. Butter 4 ramekins, then sprinkle the butter with sugar. Place the chocolate in a double boiler and melt over barely simmering water. Stir in the hazelnut paste and set aside.

In a medium saucepan, melt the butter over medium heat. Gradually stir in the polenta. Cook for 2 minutes, stirring constantly. Whisk in the milk, lower heat, and cook, stirring frequently, until thickened, about 30 minutes. Stir the chocolate mixture into the polenta. Gradually beat in the egg yolks and set aside.

In a large bowl, beat the egg whites until frothy, then gradually add the sugar while beating until stiff, glossy peaks form. Fold the beaten whites into the polenta mixture. Spoon this mixture into the prepared ramekins, filling them three-fourths full. Bake in the preheated oven for 20 to 25 minutes, or until the tops begin to split. Serve warm.

Makes 4 servings

San Domenico NY

Since its opening in 1988, Sfuzzi has been a key part of the Lincoln Center dining scene. Chef Richard Pietromonaco's casual, zesty Italian bistro fare suits a wide range of dining possibilities, including brunches, light lunches, pre-theater dinners, and full-scale sit-down dining. The restaurant's comfortable and playful setting, with its high-tech lighting, sand-blasted brick walls, and trompe l'oeil murals suggesting Roman ruins, is a piece of New York in full swing.

Sfuzzi

THE MENU
Sfuzzi

*Bruschetta with Toasted Garlic, Kalamata Olives,
and Marinated Tomatoes*

Focaccia

Tuscan White Bean and Tomato Soup

Linguine with Shrimps, Scallops, and Pesto

Cappuccino Pie

Serves Four

Bruschetta with Toasted Garlic, Kalamata Olives, and Marinated Tomatoes

Eight ½-inch-thick slices focaccia or other coarse-textured bread
2 large roasted garlic cloves (see page 206)
3 tablespoons virgin olive oil
10 Kalamata or other brine-cured black olives, pitted and roughly chopped
1 cup peeled, seeded, and diced Roma (plum) tomatoes
2 tablespoons minced fresh basil
Salt and freshly ground pepper to taste

Rub the bread slices with the garlic and brush with half of the olive oil; grill or toast them. In a medium bowl, combine the remaining olive oil, olives, tomatoes, basil, salt, and pepper. Top each slice of bread with some of this mixture and serve.

Makes 4 to 6 servings

Focaccia

1¾ cups warm milk (105° to 115°F)

1 package active dried yeast

3 tablespoons olive oil, plus more for brushing

4 to 4½ cups bread flour or unbleached all-purpose flour

1 tablespoon coarsely ground black pepper

1 teaspoon dried red pepper flakes

1 teaspoon dried rosemary

2 teaspoons dried thyme

2 teaspoons dried oregano

2 teaspoons dried basil

2 teaspoons kosher salt or to taste

To mix with a heavy-duty mixer: Place the milk, yeast, and 3 tablespoons of the olive oil in a medium bowl. Stir and let stand until the yeast is dissolved, about 10 minutes. In a large mixer bowl, using a dough hook at low speed, mix together the flour, black and red pepper, rosemary, thyme, oregano, and basil. Gradually add the milk and yeast mixture, saving a little to pick up the crumbs on the bottom of the bowl. When the dough has become an elastic, smooth ball, gradually add the salt. Continue mixing on low speed until all the salt is absorbed.

To mix by hand: Place the milk, yeast, and ½ cup of the olive oil in a very large bowl. Stir and let stand until the yeast is dissolved, about 10 minutes. Whisk in the flour ½ cup at a time until the mixture becomes too stiff for whisking, then stir in ½ cup of flour at a time with a wooden spoon. When the dough pulls away from the side of the bowl, turn it out on a lightly floured board. Knead the dough until it is smooth and elastic, 8 to 10 minutes, adding extra flour 1 tablespoon at a time as necessary to keep the dough from sticking.

Place the dough in an oiled large bowl or container and cover. Let rise in a warm place until doubled in volume, about 1 hour. Punch the dough down.

Place the dough on an unoiled 10½-by-15½-inch sheet pan or jelly roll pan and flatten to about ⅜ inch thick. Brush with olive oil and sprinkle with kosher salt. Dimple the dough with your fingers and let it rise again until doubled in volume, about 30 minutes.

Meanwhile, preheat the oven to 350°F. Bake in the preheated oven for about 30 minutes, or until golden brown. Remove from the oven and brush with olive oil. Let cool and serve the same day.

Makes one 10½-by-15½-inch focaccia

Tuscan White Bean and Tomato Soup

Cannellini are small white oval-shaped beans similar to Great Northern beans but with a thinner skin.

3 cups dried cannellini beans
2 tablespoons minced prosciutto fat or olive oil
½ onion, chopped
½ carrot, peeled and chopped
1 garlic clove, minced
1 small fresh rosemary sprig
1 fresh thyme sprig
½ bay leaf
1 cup canned tomatoes with their juice, chopped
Salt and freshly ground pepper to taste
Freshly grated Parmesan cheese for sprinkling
Extra-virgin olive oil for sprinkling

Rinse and pick through the cannellini beans. Place them in a bowl, cover with cold water, and soak overnight; drain and set aside.

In a large, heavy pot, render the prosciutto fat or heat the olive oil over medium heat. Add the onion, carrot, and garlic, and sauté until the onion is translucent, about 3 minutes. Add the rosemary, thyme, half bay leaf, tomatoes, soaked beans, and water to cover. Raise the heat to high and bring to a boil. Reduce the heat to low and simmer, stirring frequently, until the beans are tender, about 1 hour. Remove the sprigs and bay leaf. Add salt and pepper. Ladle the soup into bowls and sprinkle with Parmesan cheese and olive oil.

Makes 4 to 6 servings

Linguine with Shrimp, Scallops, and Pesto

4 quarts salted water
1 pound dried linguine
6 tablespoons olive oil
1 pound medium shrimp or rock shrimp
8 ounces sea scallops or bay scallops
¾ cup pesto (recipe follows)

In a large pot, bring the water to a boil. Add the linguine and cook at a rolling boil for 7 to 9 minutes, or until al dente, stirring occasionally to keep the pasta from sticking together.

In a large sauté pan or skillet, heat the olive oil over high heat and sauté the shrimp and scallops for 5 minutes, or until the shrimp are pink and the scallops are opaque. Stir in the pesto and remove from heat.

Drain the linguine and place in a large serving bowl. Toss together the shrimp, scallops, and pesto and serve immediately.

Makes 4 servings

Pesto

⅓ cup pine nuts
4 cups packed basil leaves
1 cup extra-virgin olive oil
2 tablespoons minced fresh garlic
1 cup (4 ounces) grated Romano or Parmesan cheese
1 tablespoon freshly ground black pepper
2 teaspoons salt

Preheat the oven to 350°F. Spread the pine nuts on a baking sheet and bake in the preheated oven until golden, 3 to 5 minutes; set aside.

In a blender or food processor, purée the basil leaves. With the motor running, slowly add the olive oil until the mixture is smooth. Add the garlic, pine nuts, cheese, and black pepper and pulse several times until the mixture is smooth but still chunky from the pine nuts. Stir in the salt and place in an airtight container. This will keep in the refrigerator for up to 2 weeks, or it may be frozen.

Makes about 2 cups

Note: Other suggested uses for pesto are as a topping for fresh mozzarella and tomato salad, a spread for grilled bread, a sauce for pasta, and a pizza topping.

Cappuccino Pie

1½ cups chocolate cookie crumbs
½ cup (1 stick) butter at room temperature
6 cups vanilla bean gelato
3 tablespoons coffee extract or cold brewed espresso
⅓ cup semisweet chocolate shavings

In a medium bowl, combine the cookie crumbs and butter. Press the mixture evenly and firmly into an unbuttered 9-inch springform pan.

In a large bowl, defrost the vanilla bean gelato until soft. Stir in the coffee extract and the chocolate shavings. Pour the mixture into the prepared pan, cover with plastic wrap, and place immediately in the freezer. Remove from the pan and cut into slices; serve frozen.

Makes one 9-inch pie; serves 8 to 10

Sfuzzi

Renowned as one of the most beautiful restaurants in New York, the Sign of the Dove has been a family affair since it was opened by Dr. Joseph Santo in 1962; daily management duties are now fulfilled by his brother and sister-in-law, Berge and Henny Santo. Located on the corner of East 65th Street and Third Avenue, the restaurant's dove symbol recalls a time when this part of Manhattan's Upper East Side was known as Dove Lots, and the neighborhood tavern was indeed at the sign of a dove.

The Sign of the Dove's fundamentally Provençal menu also is influenced by Morocco, Thailand, Italy, and America. American-trained chef Andrew D'Amico emphasizes the diversity of ingredients available in multiethnic New York more than any one culinary tradition in his thoughtfully orchestrated menus that change with the season. The restaurant's wine cellar has remarkable depth in great names and includes rare bottles from John F. Kennedy's cellar.

The Sign of the Dove does many things well simultaneously, offering à la carte and fixed-price dining, a café menu, meals for large and diverse business functions, weekend brunches with music, and upscale retail baking.

Sign of the Dove

THE MENU
The Sign of the Dove

Sea Scallops with Broccoli Rabe and Curry Sauce

Veal Loin with Caramelized Onions, Poached Pears,
and Cabernet Syrup

Gratin of Potatoes and Leeks

Orange Crème Brûlée Tart

Serves Four

Sea Scallops with Broccoli Rabe and Curry Sauce

Broccoli rabe has a pungent and slightly bitter taste that adds zest to this elegant appetizer.

Curry Sauce
4 tablespoons olive oil
1 small leek, chopped
1 apple or pear, peeled, cored, and chopped
5 shallots, minced
½ small onion, chopped
1 celery stalk, chopped
2 garlic cloves, chopped
½ mango or papaya, cored or seeded and chopped
1½ tablespoons Madras curry powder
¼ teaspoon coriander seeds
¼ teaspoon white peppercorns
2 cups Chardonnay or other dry white wine
2 cups fish stock (see page 204), chicken stock (see page 202), or
    canned low-salt chicken broth
¼ cup heavy (whipping) cream
1 tablespoon butter
Salt and freshly ground pepper to taste

1¼ pounds sea scallops
Salt and freshly ground pepper to taste
Vegetable oil for sautéing
1 pound broccoli rabe
2 tablespoons minced fresh chives for garnish

To make the sauce: In a large nonaluminum pan, heat 2 tablespoons of the oil over medium heat, add the leek, apple or pear, shallots, onion, celery, garlic, and mango or papaya, and sauté for 10 minutes. Add the curry powder,

Sign of the Dove

coriander seeds, and peppercorns, and cook 2 minutes longer. Add the wine, raise heat to high, and cook to reduce the liquid by two thirds. Add the fish or chicken stock or broth and cook to reduce the liquid again by half. Reduce the heat to low, add the cream, and simmer 5 minutes more. Whisk in the butter and add salt and pepper. Strain through fine-meshed sieve, pressing down on the solids with the back of a spoon; discard the solids and set the curry sauce aside.

Bring a large saucepan of salted water to a boil, add the broccoli rabe, and cook for 4 to 5 minutes, or until crisp-tender; drain and keep warm.

Meanwhile, rinse the scallops, pat them dry with paper towels, and sprinkle them with salt and pepper. Film a heavy sauté pan or skillet with vegetable oil, heat over medium-high heat, and sauté the scallops until they are very lightly browned, about 2 minutes on each side.

To serve, mound some of the broccoli rabe in the center of each plate and arrange the scallops around it. Spoon the sauce between the scallops and garnish with chopped chives.

Makes 4 servings

Veal Loin with Caramelized Onions, Poached Pears, and Cabernet Syrup

3 tablespoons coarsely chopped mixed fresh herbs such as oregano, parsley,
   rosemary, sage, and thyme

3 tablespoons olive oil

2 garlic cloves, sliced

2 pounds veal loin or tenderloin, trimmed, with silver skin removed

1½ tablespoons vegetable oil

2 pounds onions (about 4), thinly sliced

Coarse salt and freshly ground black pepper to taste

Poached Pears and Cabernet Syrup

2 cups Cabernet Sauvignon

⅓ cup sugar

One 2-inch piece cinnamon stick

2 cloves

1 small dried red chili

1½ tablespoons black peppercorns

2 Bosc pears, peeled, halved, and cored

In a small bowl, combine the herbs, olive oil, and garlic. Rub this mixture into the veal, cover, and refrigerate for 6 to 12 hours.

In a large sauté pan or skillet, heat the vegetable oil over medium heat and sauté the onions until they are golden, 20 to 25 minutes; keep warm.

Meanwhile, prepare the poached pears and Cabernet syrup: In an 8-cup saucepan, bring the wine, sugar, cinnamon, cloves, chili, and peppercorns to a boil. Reduce heat to low, add the pears, and simmer for 20 minutes. Using a slotted spoon, carefully remove the pears let cool.

Continue to simmer the liquid until it reduces somewhat, then pour it into a smaller pan and simmer until it becomes thick and syrupy. Set aside and let cool. Dice the pears and set them aside.

Preheat the oven to 400°F. Remove the meat from the refrigerator and let sit at room temperature for at least 30 minutes. Sprinkle the meat with salt and pepper, and sear it for about 3 minutes on each side in a cast-iron pan over high heat or on a grill over hot coals. Place the meat in a roasting pan and bake in the preheated oven for about 1 hour and 15 minutes, or until it reaches an internal temperature of 165° to 170°F.

Transfer the veal to a platter and let rest for 3 to 5 minutes before slicing it across the grain. Divide the slices among 6 warmed plates. Garnish with some caramelized onions, poached pears, and the Cabernet syrup.

Makes 6 servings

Gratin of Potatoes and Leeks

4 russet potatoes
1 cup milk
1 cup water
Salt to taste
2 tablespoons unsalted butter at room temperature
1 cup diced leeks
1/2 cup soft bread crumbs
Freshly grated nutmeg to taste
Freshly ground pepper to taste
2 tablespoons truffle oil (available in specialty foods stores), optional
1 cup heavy (whipping) cream
1 cup (4 ounces) grated Cheddar or Gruyère cheese
1/4 cup grated Parmesan cheese

Peel and thinly slice the potatoes. Place the potatoes, milk, and water in a medium saucepan. Season with salt and bring to a boil. Simmer for 10 to 15 minutes, or until the potatoes are tender but not falling apart. Drain the potatoes and spread the slices out in a flat pan to cool.

In a medium sauté pan or skillet, melt 1 tablespoon of the butter over medium-low heat and sauté the leeks until soft but not browned. Butter a 9-inch ovenproof dish with the remaining 1 tablespooon butter and coat evenly with the bread crumbs.

Evenly distribute one third of the potatoes over the bottom of the baking dish. Season with nutmeg, salt, and pepper and drizzle the optional truffle oil over the top. Pour 1/3 cup of the cream over the potatoes. Top with a layer of half of the sautéed leeks and half of the cheese.

Place the second layer of another third of the potatoes on top, press down gently, and repeat the layers of seasoning, cream, leeks, and cheese. Distribute the remaining potato slices evenly over the top, season with salt and pepper,

Sign of the Dove

and sprinkle with the Parmesan cheese. Pour the remaining 1/3 cup cream over the top. You may assemble, cover, and refrigerate the gratin for up to ten hours before baking.

Preheat the oven to 400°F. Place the baking dish on a baking pan to avoid spillage onto the oven. Bake for 20 minutes, or until the top is browned and the center is bubbling. Let cool briefly and serve.

Makes 4 servings

Orange Crème Brûlée Tart

Pastry

2½ cups unbleached all-purpose flour

¼ cup sugar

2 cups (4 sticks) cold butter, cut into small pieces

3 egg yolks

3 tablespoons heavy (whipping) cream

Orange Custard

Juice and zest of 4 oranges

2 tablespoons Grand Marnier

2½ cups heavy (whipping) cream

1 vanilla bean, split lengthwise

8 egg yolks

7 tablespoons sugar

½ cup sour cream

Sugar for dusting

Raspberry coulis (see page 205)

Fresh berries for garnish

To make the pastry: Place the flour and sugar in a medium bowl. Using a pastry cutter or 2 knives, cut the butter into the flour and sugar until crumbly, being careful not to overmix. Stir in the egg yolks and cream. Press the dough into a ball, cover with plastic wrap, and chill for 1 hour before rolling out.

Preheat the oven to 350°F. On a lightly floured work surface, roll out the pastry to a 10-inch circle ⅛ inch thick. Fit the pastry into an 8-inch spring-form pan or pie pan. Crimp the edges of the pastry and prick the bottom with a fork. Fit a piece of aluminum foil into the pastry and weigh it down with pie weights, dried beans, or rice. Bake the pastry in the preheated oven for 15 to 20 minutes, or until it is lightly browned on the edges. Remove and let cool.

To make the orange custard: In a medium saucepan, cook the orange juice,

Sign of the Dove

orange zest, and Grand Marnier over medium heat until the alcohol is burned off, about 3 minutes. Add the cream and vanilla bean and cook at a gentle boil until the liquid has reduced by a third.

In a double boiler over barely simmering water, whisk the egg yolks and 7 tablespoons of the sugar until the mixture thickens enough so that a slowly dissolving ribbon is formed on the surface when the whisk is lifted. Add the reduced orange mixture and whisk until it thickens enough to coat the back of a spoon. Remove from heat and whisk in the sour cream. Let cool and pour into the pastry shell. Cover and place in the freezer for several hours until frozen.

Thirty minutes before serving, preheat the broiler. Remove the tart from the freezer and dust the top with a layer of granulated sugar. Place the tart under the broiler for 20 or 30 seconds, or until the sugar is nicely caramelized. Refrigerate until just before serving. Slice and serve with raspberry coulis and fresh berries.

Makes one 8-inch tart; serves 6 to 8

Sign of the Dove

Basics

Beef, Veal, or Chicken Glaze

Cook beef, veal, chicken stock, or canned low-salt chicken broth over high heat until the liquid is reduced to a syrupy consistency. Meat glaze will keep in the refrigerator for several weeks.

Beef Stock

4 pounds meaty sliced beef shanks
2 tablespoons olive oil
1 onion, chopped
1 carrot, peeled and chopped
1 celery stalk, chopped
1 bay leaf
3 sprigs parsley
6 black peppercorns
½ cup dry white wine
3 quarts water
½ cup tomato purée
Salt and pepper to taste

Preheat the oven to 400°F. In a roasting pan, toss the bones with the olive oil. Brown for 30 to 40 minutes, turning occasionally. Transfer the bones to a large saucepan or kettle.

Pour the fat out of the roasting pan, and deglaze the pan with the wine. Pour this liquid into the saucepan or kettle with the rest of the ingredients. Bring to a boil and skim off any foam that rises to the top. Simmer slowly for 3 to 4 hours, adding more water if necessary to maintain the original level.

Strain through a sieve into a bowl and refrigerate. Remove any congealed fat that rises to the surface. This stock will keep for 3 days in a covered container

201

in the refrigerator. To keep longer, bring to a boil every 3 days. To freeze, pour into a plastic container and seal well.

Makes about 1 quart

Clarified Butter

In a heavy saucepan, melt butter over low heat until it bubbles. Remove the pan from heat and carefully skim off the foamy butterfat that has risen to the surface. Pour the clear yellow liquid into a container, leaving the milky residue at the bottom; cover. Clarified butter will keep for months in the refrigerator or freezer.

Chicken Stock

About 8 cups chopped raw and/or cooked chicken bones and scraps
2 teaspoons salt
1 onion, chopped
1 carrot, peeled and chopped
3 celery stalks, chopped
8 parsley sprigs
Salt and freshly ground pepper to taste

Place the bones and scraps in a large stockpot. Add water to cover by 1 inch and the salt. Bring to a slow boil, simmering off any foam that rises to the surface. Add the onion, celery, carrots, and parsley. Cover the pan, reduce heat, and simmer for 1 hour, adding water as necessary to keep the ingredients covered. Season with salt and pepper. Strain through a sieve into a large bowl and refrigerate. Scrape off any surface fat that congeals on top.

Makes about 8 cups

Note: This stock will keep 3 to 4 days in a covered container in the refrigerator.

Basics

To keep it longer, bring it to a boil every 3 to 4 days. To freeze, pour into a plastic container and seal well; chicken stock will keep for 2 months in the refrigerator.

Court Bouillon

2 cups water
4 parsley sprigs
2 celery leaves
1 bay leaf
¼ teaspoon freshly ground black pepper
Pinch of fennel seed or aniseed
½ small onion, cut into quarters
½ cup dry white wine, or 2 tablespoons fresh lemon juice

In a medium saucepan, bring all the ingredients to a boil and simmer for 20 minutes. Remove from heat and strain through a sieve; set aside.

Makes about 2 cups

Crème Fraîche

The advantage of crème fraîche over sour cream is that it can be boiled and reduced without curdling. It will keep in the refrigerator for about 1 week.

1 cup heavy (whipping) cream
2 tablespoons buttermilk or yogurt

Combine the ingredients in a glass container and let sit at room temperature (70° to 80°F) for 5 to 8 hours or overnight to thicken. Refrigerate in a covered container.

Makes 1 cup

Fish Stock

About 4 cups fish heads, bones, and trimmings
1 celery stalk, chopped
1 onion, chopped
1 carrot, peeled and chopped
1 bay leaf
4 parsley sprigs
Salt and pepper to taste

Rinse the fish parts. In a large stockpot, place the fish parts, celery, onion, carrot, bay leaf, parsley, and water to cover by 1 inch. Bring to a boil and skim off the foam as it rises to the surface. Cover and simmer for 20 minutes. Remove from the heat and strain through a sieve. Adjust the seasoning with salt and pepper. Store the cooled stock in a covered container for 2 days in the refrigerator and 2 months in the freezer. To refrigerate longer, bring the stock to a boil every 2 days.

Makes about 4 cups

Garlic Olive Oil

2 cups olive oil
3 garlic cloves, crushed

Add the olive oil and garlic to a medium saucepan. Heat over low heat until the mixture is fragrant and just warm to the touch. Let cool. Pour the oil into a bottle with the garlic; seal and store indefinitely.

Makes 2 cups

Garlic Toast
8 slices coarse-textured bread, cut ½-inch thick
4 garlic cloves, halved
8 tablespoons extra-virgin olive oil
Salt and freshly ground pepper to taste

Basics

Toast the bread slices, and while still warm rub each slice with the cut side of a garlic clove. Drizzle a tablespoon of olive oil over each slice. Season with salt and pepper.

Makes 8 slices

Peeling Hazelnuts

Preheat the oven to 350°F. Spread the nuts on a baking sheet or in a jelly-roll pan and bake for 10 to 15 minutes or until lightly browned, stirring once or twice. Remove from the oven, fold in a kitchen towel, and rub with the towel to remove the skins. Pour the nuts into a colander and shake it over the sink to discard remaining skins.

Peeling and Seeding Tomatoes

Remove the cores from the tomatoes and cut an X in the opposite ends. Drop the tomatoes into a pot of rapidly boiling water for 3 to 4 seconds, or until the skin by the X peels away slightly. Drain and run cold water over the tomatoes; the skin should slip off easily. To seed, cut the tomatoes in half crosswise, hold each half upside down over the sink, and gently squeeze and shake to remove the seeds.

Raspberry Coulis

2 cups fresh raspberries, or one 10-ounce package frozen unsweetened
    raspberries, defrosted
Powdered sugar to taste
1 tablespoon kirsch, or to taste

Place all the ingredients in a blender or a food processor and purée until smooth.

Makes 2 cups

Roasted Garlic

1 whole head garlic
1 tablespoon olive oil
Salt and freshly ground pepper to taste

Preheat the oven to 350°F. Using a sharp knife, trim the roots from the garlic head and cut off the top of the bulb, exposing the individual garlic cloves. Place the bulb root-side-down in a shallow baking pan. Drizzle with the olive oil, season lightly with salt and pepper, and cover tightly with aluminum foil. Bake in the oven for 1½ hours, or until the garlic softens.

To Section Citrus Fruit

Cut off the top and bottom of an orange, grapefruit, or lemon down to the flesh, then stand the fruit upright and cut off the peel in sections down to the flesh. Working over a bowl to catch the juice, hold the fruit in one hand and cut between the membranes. Rotate the fruit and let the sections fall into the bowl. Pick out any seeds.

Toasting Almonds

Preheat the oven to 350°F. Spread the almonds on a baking sheet and bake for 8 to 10 minutes or until very lightly browned, stirring once or twice. Whole roasted nuts may be stored in an airtight container in the refrigerator or freezer.

Tomato Concassée

Cut the pulp from a peeled, and seeded tomato into neat dice.

Veal Stock

2 pounds meaty sliced veal shanks
2 tablespoons oil
1 onion, chopped
1 carrot, peeled and chopped
1 celery stalk, chopped
½ cup dry white wine
Salt and pepper to taste

Preheat the oven to 400 F. In a roasting pan, toss the bones with the oil and vegetables. Brown for 30 to 40 minutes, turning occasionally. Transfer the bones and vegetables to a large saucepan or kettle.

Pour the fat out of the roasting pan, and deglaze the pan with the wine. Pour this liquid into the saucepan with the bones and vegetables. Add water to cover the ingredients by 1 inch. Bring to a boil and skim off any foam that rises to the top. Add salt and pepper, cover, and simmer 3 to 4 hours.

Strain through a sieve into a bowl and refrigerate. Remove any congealed fat that rises to the surface. This stock will keep for 3 days in a covered container in the refrigerator. To keep longer, bring to a boil every 3 days. To freeze, pour into a plastic container and seal well; veal stock will keep for 2 months in the freezer.

Makes about 1 quart

Veal Glaze

Place 1 quart veal stock (see above) in a saucepan and bring to a boil. Reduce to 1 cup by boiling over medium-low heat, until a thick, very flavorful amber syrup forms. This will solidify to a very firm jelly when chilled. This jelly can then be cut into eight one-ounce squares, wrapped individually, and frozen.

White Veal Stock

2 pounds sliced meaty veal shanks
2 tablespoons oil
1 onion, chopped
1 carrot, peeled and chopped
1 celery stalk, chopped
½ cup dry white wine
Salt and freshly ground black pepper to taste

Place the veal shanks and water to cover by 1 inch in a large stockpot. Bring to a boil, skimming off any foam that rises to the top. Add the remaining ingredients to the stockpot. Cover and simmer for 3 to 4 hours.

Strain through a fine-meshed sieve into a large bowl and refrigerate until the fat on the surface has congealed. Remove and discard the fat. This stock will keep for up to 3 to 4 days in a covered container in the refrigerator. To keep it longer, bring it to a boil every 3 to 4 days. To freeze, pour into a plastic container, seal well, and freeze for up to 2 months.

Makes about 4 cups

Conversion Charts

Weight Measurements

Standard U.S.	Ounces	Metric
1 ounce	1	30 g
¼ lb	4	125 g
½ lb	8	250 g
1 lb	16	500 g
1½ lb	24	750 g
2 lb	32	1 kg
2½ lb	40	1.25 kg
3 lb	48	1.5 kg

Volume Measurements

Standard U.S.	Ounces	Metric
1 tbs	½	15 ml
2 tbs	1	30 ml
3 tbs	1½	45 ml
¼ cup (4 tbs)	2	60 ml
6 tbs	3	90 ml
½ cup (8 tbs)	4	125 ml
1 cup	8	250 ml
1 pint (2 cups)	16	500 ml
4 cups	32	1 L

Oven Temperatures

Fahrenheit	Celsius
300°	150°
325°	165°
350°	180°
375°	190°
400°	200°
425°	220°
450°	230°

Conversion Factors

Ounces to grams: Multiply the ounce figure by 28.3 to get the number of grams.

Pounds to grams: Multiply the pound figure by 453.59 to get the number of grams.

Pounds to kilograms: Multiply the pound figure by 0.45 to get the number of kilograms.

Ounces to milliliters: Multiply the ounce figure by 30 to get the number of milliliters.

Cups to liters: Multiply the cup figure by 0.24 to get the number of liters.

Fahrenheit to Celsius: Subtract 32 from the Fahrenheit figure, multiply by 5, then divide by 9 to get the Celsius figure.

List of Restaurants

An American Place
2 Park Avenue
New York, NY 10016
(212) 684-2122

Bice
7 East 54th Street
New York, NY 10022
(212) 688-1999

Café des Artistes
One West 67th Street
New York, NY 10023
(212) 877-3500

Chanterelle
2 Harrison Street
New York, NY 10013
(212) 966-6960

Felidia Ristorante
243 East 58th Street
New York, NY 10022
(212) 758-1479

The Four Seasons
99 East 52nd Street
New York, NY 10022
(212) 754-9494

Il Cantinori
32 East Tenth Street
New York, NY 10003
(212) 673-6044

Il Monello
1460 Second Avenue
New York, NY 10021
(212) 535-9310

La Caravelle
33 West 55th Street
New York, NY 10019
(212) 586-4252

La Côte Basque
5 East 55th Street
New York, NY 10022
(212) 688-6525

Le Bernardin
155 West 51st Street
New York, NY 10019
(212) 489-1515

Le Cirque
58 East 65th Street
New York, NY 10021
(212) 794-9292

Lutèce
249 East 50th Street
New York, NY 10022
(212) 752-2225

Mark's Restaurant
25 East 77th Street
New York, NY 10021
(212) 879-1864

Palio
151 West 51st Street
New York, NY 10019
(212) 245-4850

Parioli Romanissimo
24 East 81st Street
New York, NY 10028
(212) 288-2391

Petrossian Restaurant
182 West 58th Street
New York, NY 10019
(212) 245-2214

Primavera
1578 First Avenue
New York, NY 10028
(212) 861-8608

San Domenico NY
240 Central Park South
New York, NY 10019
(212) 265-5959

Sfuzzi
58 West 65th Street
New York, NY 10023
(212) 873-3700

The Sign of the Dove
1110 Third Avenue
New York, NY 10021
(212) 861-8080

Acknowledgments

I would like to thank all the many people who made this volume possible.

Special thanks are due to Andrew Heyden of the Metropolitan Opera Guild for suggesting this project in the first place and for all his help during the past year. I am forever grateful to Paul Gruber for his expertise and assistance with the musical selections. Thanks also to recording engineer George Horn for the digital remastering, and to Donna Malyszko, Felicia Gearhart, and Kelly Burns.

My deepest gratitude to the proprietors and chefs of the restaurants who generously contributed menus and recipes to the cookbook: Larry Forgione, Kevin Dwyer, Roberto Ruggeri, Paul Gozzardo, Martel Mattei, Jerry Goldman, George Lang, Jenifer Lang, David Waltuck, Karen Waltuck, Felice Bastianich, Lidia Bastianich, Paul Kovi, Tom Margittai, Hitsch Albin, Regina McMenamin, Frank Minieri, Steve Tzolis, Nicola Kotsoni, Adi Giovanetti, Rosanna Giovanetti, Andrea Lorenzi, André Jammet, Rita Jammet, Tadashi Ono, Laurent Richard, Jean Jacques Rachou, Sirio Maccioni, Sylvain Portay, Jacques Torres, Gilbert LeCoze, Eric Ripert, Herve Poussot, André Soltner, Simone Soltner, Raymond Bickson, Erik Maillard, Jean-Luc Deguines, Maria Pia Hellrigl, Hans Kaufmann, Rubrio Rossi, Suzanne Rossi, Robin Hollis, Joseph Pace, Nicola Civetta, Peggy Civetta, Tony May, Theo Schoenegger, William Trimmer, Richard Pietromonaco, Dr. Joseph Santo, Berge Santo, Henny Santo, and Andrew D'Amico. Thanks also to the staffs of the restaurants for prompt assistance.

I am so glad to have had Carolyn Miller as my editor once again; thank you for your attention to detail, expert advice, and culinary insights. Grateful acknowledgments are due to Jim Armstrong, Steve Patterson, and Ned Waring, who contributed in many ways, and to the rest of the staff at Menus and Music. Thanks to Carolina Chincarini for the Italian translations. Michael Osborne and Tom Kamegai deserve many thanks for their wonderful design and enthusiastic support of this project. I especially want to thank my daughters Claire and Caitlin and my husband John for their encouragement and their love.

Index

Index

214

215

Index

Index

217

Index

Sharon O'Connor is a musician, author, and cook. She also is the founder of the San Francisco String Quartet and creator of the *Menus and Music* series, which combines her love of music and food. *Dining and the Opera in Manhattan* is the ninth volume in her series of cookbooks with musical recordings.